GANGLAND GLASGOW

By the same author:

Glasgow's Hard Men

Glasgow's Godfather

The Wee Book of the Clyde

*

The Herald Book of the Clyde

Doon the Watter

Clydeside, People and Places

Images of Glasgow

Scotland's Sporting Heroes

(all with Ian Watson)

GANGLAND GLASGOW

TRUE CRIME FROM THE STREETS

ROBERT JEFFREY

BLACK & WHITE PUBLISHING

First published 2002
by Black & White Publishing Ltd
99 Giles Street, Edinburgh EH6 6BZ

Reprinted 2003, 2004, 2005

ISBN 1 902927 59 1

Photographs courtesy of The Scottish Daily Record
and the SMG Photographic Archive

Printed and bound by Creative Print and Design

CONTENTS

ACKNOWLEDGEMENTS

I would like to acknowledge the assistance in the production of this book of Marie Jeffrey, Samantha Boyd, Rod Ramsay, Stuart Jeffrey, Ian Watson, the library staff of the Scottish Media Group, Elizabeth Carmichael and the friendly and efficient staff of the Glasgow Room in the Mitchell Library, Catherine Torretti of the *Daily Record* and the senior researcher Stroma Fraser, a Scots/Australian librarian whose enthusiasm is both enormous and infectious and whose expertise was invaluable.

RJ
Carradale, Argyll

1

GLASGOW SPRING

Glaswegians' view of their city was cruelly jolted back to reality in the spring of 2002. Suddenly violence had reappeared on the agenda. The renaissance brought about by the Year of Culture, the Garden Festival, the new Concert Hall, the Burrell collection and the seemingly unstoppable growth of bookshops, trendy restaurants and pavement café life was somewhat overshadowed by dramatic events on the streets.

The return to the bad old days of inter-gang warfare, of evil factions fighting for power and turf and settling old scores in the nastiest of ways, was particularly shocking simply because for many years much of the reporting of it had largely dropped out of newspapers.

The citizens of the Dear Green Place had begun to believe their own publicity a little too much. The old city, now with the grime of tenement walls blasted away, and new exciting city centre and riverside architecture providing a superficial gloss, was, however, shown to be not as far removed from its old reputation as something akin to a Chicago of far north west Europe as the douce burghers had grown to believe.

In April and May the fashionable caffe latte-sippers had their attention jolted from the latest pontificating arts reviews that take up so much space in the city's papers these days, and found themselves once again reading of the doings of old-fashioned gangsters. The concept of these new battles for power is little different from the past. But the style of the warriors is far removed from that of the gangsters of the twenties or thirties or indeed the hoodlums and corner boy gangs of the seventies and eighties. Control of the drugs trade has become, for the major gangs, the main driving force. There are still battles in the schemes between small groups of youths staking claim to territory and fighting over their molls. Indeed there is a massive upsurge in knife-related crime across Scotland, not just in Glasgow. In the cliché of the tabloids, "blade culture" is on the way back.

But if knife-carrying and booze and drug-fuelled rumbles at the weekend is a return to old ways, it is rather different for the major players in gangland. Now the gangster is no longer a sad-looking loner in a sleazy bar with his pallid "chib"-marked face showing him to be a man of many disputes, perhaps mad, perhaps bad, but certainly dangerous to tangle with.

The hoodlum of the twenty-first century presents a different face to the public. Even if the city still had its famous shoogly trams you can be sure he would not be taking them, even to ride about the streets of the east end where so much blood has been spilled over the years.

The preferred method of transport for the big boys these days is the 4x4 recreational vehicle, heavily chromed and as powerful as possible. Never mind that such a status symbol of a vehicle is destined never to muddy a tyre with off-road excursions other than a quick trip up a rutted and unlighted back alley where a little business might be done.

Behind the wheel will be a man with the expected gold jewellery dripping from every visible part of his body. His suits are designer gear bought with no thought to expense and some would say even less to taste. One item of clothing though is shockingly standard – a bullet proof vest.

The home of such a man is mostly likely be an expensive pile in a desirable suburb. The days when godfathers lived in a tenement flat surrounded by the people whose lives they bilked and blighted are long gone. The house will perhaps be decorated in a style not familiar to the neighbours. But the neighbours in the leafy avenues will note with little surprise that the boot of the four wheel drive recreational vehicle contains an expensive set of golf clubs.

These clubs may be standard equipment, with top of the range labels and built to the approval of the regulations of the Royal and Ancient Golf Club of St Andrews, but they are not solely for use on the manicured fairways of the elitist clubs of the West of Scotland. They are a designer weapon for the new street warrior.

One gang member interviewed in the late sixties mentioned a number of weapons . . . hatchets, hammers, knives, meat cleavers, meat hooks, bayonets, machetes, open razors, sharp-tailed combs, bottles, tumblers, bricks and sticks. It was a sign of less sophisticated criminal times that this particular young street fighter omitted to mention firearms. However to that fearsome list of gangland weaponry can now be added golf clubs as well as guns.

The golf clubs have the added advantage that when the owner is stopped by some inquisitive, and brave, cop they can easily be explained away: just popping down the coast for a few holes, officer.

A whack over the head with a nine iron can do some considerable damage and is hard to forgive or forget. And forgetting is a concept that down the years the Glasgow gangster has had extreme difficulty in accepting. The merest slight lingers on in the memory as a score that some day must be settled.

The spring 2002 outbreak of highly visible street violence appears to have started when Tam McGraw, a man alleged to lead a gang faction, and despite always denying wrongdoing, considered by some to be a contender for the criminal accolade of Godfather in succession to such as Walter Norval and Arthur Thompson, was allegedly attacked by a knife-wielding assailant in the street in daylight. McGraw, aka The Licensee to everyone in the east end where he once ran a notorious bar called the Caravel, leads an interesting life style. His sobriquet may come from his bar-owning background or, as his enemies would claim, because he is alleged to have a licence to operate. It is a matter of much debate.

In 1988 he was accused of bank rolling a major drug-running

operation and stood trial in Edinburgh, defended by perhaps Scotland's current most famous pleader Donald Findlay Q.C. The trial was a lengthy, expensive affair lasting fifty-five days. But at the end of it Thomas McGraw walked free after the jury returned a not proven verdict.

His release came after a masterful performance by the flamboyant Q.C. who had told the court that his client was an Arthur Daley figure, ducking and diving, but that there was not one scrap of evidence to link his money with the buying of drugs in Spain.

Mr McGraw, infamously a man of few words, was not moved on this occasion, by his court room success, to break the habit of a lifetime. Asked for a comment by reporters he told them to "f*** off" and disappeared from the scene in his black Mercedes.

The source of his wealth had been discussed in court by Mr Findlay, who talked of his legitimate activities, a cash and carry business, ice cream vans and the aforementioned Caravel pub.

It was the police belief that the customers in this particular howff discussed much thuggery and lawbreaking. Anyone brave enough to be thinking of a quick tourist trip to gawp at a legendary underworld site and enjoy a sip of the amber nectar in the company of some seriously no-good citizens can forget it. The Caravel is no more – bulldozed in mysterious circumstances. Underworld informers had suggested to the police that customers might have had a role in the infamous deaths of Joe "Bananas" Hanlon and Bobby Glover, who were found shot dead in a car on the day of the funeral of Arthur Thompson's son Fat Boy. But after the demolition, forensic examination of the premises was not possible, and an avenue of inquiry, as the police might say, was closed forever.

The lifestyle of this particular Glasgow business man is reported to include driving a luxury Japanese 4x4, a home in the sunshine of Tenerife, property interests in Ireland and a house in the Mount Vernon district said to be worth more than £300,000.

Initial reports said he was badly injured in the attack, but one thing is for sure – the wise precaution of wearing a bullet-proof vest saved him from more serious injury. The Kevlar coat worked its magic and the injuries, which turned out to be relatively minor, were patched up in the private Ross Hall hospital in Crookston, a place more commonly used to monitor the heartbeats of worried stockbrokers than give succour to victims of knife attacks in the street.

All this renewed spilling of bad blood is part of an interlocking jigsaw of hard men who know each other and are in a battle for power.

According to some reports the man The Licensee was brawling with was Paul Ferris, a former adjutant of McGraw's. At the time Ferris was not long out of jail after serving a sentence for gun running. But he soon found himself briefly back behind bars for allegedly breaching his parole regulations. The safety of a return to prison could have been a welcome, if temporary, respite, for Paul Ferris has many enemies in the city and the "word on the streets" was that there was a contract out on him.

Ferris had been released early in 2002 from Durham jail after serving four years of a seven-year sentence. Back in Glasgow he immediately made a series of TV and newspaper interviews in which he pledged to go straight. He even co-authored a novel which drew heavily on his earlier life as a villain. Unsurprisingly the declarations of turning over the proverbial new leaf were greeted by the police and his associates and rivals with serious scepticism.

As in the past, this criminal côterie, involving Ferris, the infamous Barlanark Team and the remnants of Arthur Thompson's army, are well known to the police who have on occasion said, off the record, that the sight of drug barons taking each other out is not a problem.

But after the new trouble on the streets and a high profile return to jail, Ferris was released as there was said to be no reason to hold him longer. No talk of breaching parole regulations. Later we will return to the fall out from that decision and the new battles and intrigues of big-time crime in Glasgow in the twenty-first century.

As in all criminal societies, the hoods of Glasgow have their own strange codes which survive the passing of the years, a regular supply of new chief constables and new anti-crime initiatives of all sorts.

Friends fall out and friendships are reformed. There are some remarkable instances of this. For example, a security guard – a business claimed by some to be infiltrated with gangsters using it as a front – likes to tell the tale over a pint or six of a couple of school friends who fell into dispute. One knifed the other who went on to get a few thousand pounds in compensation. The episode with the blade notwithstanding, the two made up and when the "compo" arrived, the victim was so pally with his one-time assailant that he donated half the cash to him!

In true Mafia style much of this sort of friendship is about "respect". Interestingly about the time all this was happening in Glasgow, the legendary Joe Bonanno died in Arizona at the age of ninety-seven, which is remarkable considering the life he led. Proof that the bad guys sometimes survive longer than you would expect. Like Arthur Thompson, Glasgow's most famous Godfather – or business man as he liked to style himself – Bonanno died of a heart attack. 'Joe Bananas' trade was narcotics, gambling and pornography, and it was helped along the way with a strategic murder or two, including the ordering of the killing of an old friend of his father. He rose to head five New York Mafia families.

But his request for "respect" was merely the call of the Glasgow gangster writ large. He was in his own eyes "a man of honour". It is impossible to underestimate the ego of such men. Joe Bananas actually called a book he wrote "Man of Honour" and then tried to sue his publisher, claiming that he was portrayed on the cover as a "cheap gangster".

Bonanno might have been out of the headlines for some time, but not long after he died came the demise of another worldwide gang legend, John Gotti. The Dapper Don, as he was known, also died in his bed – from cancer. But this time the bed was in a prison hospital where the man who was the most famous American gangster since Al Capone found himself after a murder trial.

Intriguingly the events on the New York streets brought to mind the High Court trial of Glasgow Godfather Walter Norval, when the court was fire bombed in an attempt to stop the trial by destroying documents and scaring witnesses. Much the same happened in the States at the Gotti trial and there was a plethora of bomb scares, absent defendants, allegations of witness intimidation and even the murder of an associate whose car was blown up. Anywhere gangsters run, the police face the problems of witnesses too scared to talk. A classic example of this involved Gotti, when a stabbing victim overstayed his time in hospital and when finally appearing on the stand found himself surprisingly unable to identify his assailant, Gotti. "I Forgotti" said a classic headline in the *New York Daily News* the next day.

In another remarkable escape from the clutches of the law, Gotti was accused of assaulting a union official. He told the arresting officer "I'll lay you three to one I beat it". He did. Helped along the way by the fact that the victim who had been shot four times gave evidence for the defence!

Gotti finally went to the cells for a long stretch for his part in the murder of a rival, Paul "Big Paulie" Castellano. Interestingly the role of drugs and the morality of the gangs in dealing played a part. Gotti's mentor, a gent with the name of Aneillo "Mr Neil" Dellacroce, was an adherent of the old Mafia rule of "You Deal, You Die". The new regime soon blew away "Big Paulie" and "Mr Neil".

The thousand dollar suits, the diamond rings and the mane of silver hair put Gotti on to the front cover of *Time* magazine and fed a giant ego. And it is hard not to conclude that ego as well as greed has played a role in the recent eruption of gangland violence in Glasgow. So-called Tartan Mafia "men of honour" are at war. Old scores are being settled.

Around the same time as the attack on The Licensee, Thomas "TC" Campbell was attacked by a man wielding a golf club. "TC" was at the time free pending an appeal on his life sentence for his role in the killing of the Doyle family in the so-called Ice Cream Wars of the early eighties.

All this recent activity has flushed to the surface the unwanted truth that Glasgow is still a violent city, a place which once had a murder rate higher than that of Palermo.

East end of London villain turned journalist, John McVicar, pointed out that particular comparison and the city's preference for "making trouble rather than money". But it was also stated that in the local drug trade the violence was less personal, more business-like. Drug outlets and territories were defended in blood, a truth that can be confirmed by any Glasgow cop or court reporter.

Despite this, down the years, many in high places in the city have failed to face facts. The pretence that there are no gang wars, no history of violence, is absurd. But, like the holocaust, Glasgow's gang wars have their share of deniers, even to this day. The fact that most of the violence in the city does not impinge directly on many in the pleasant suburbs and the palm-potted Merchant City flats with their terraces and white and chrome minimalist interior design, does not mean the drug problem and the gang problem has gone away or is going away.

Right from the days of Alexander McArthur's *No Mean City* there have been those who have denied even a grain of truth in that novel and its portrayal of gang violence in the Gorbals. Plays and films on Jimmy Boyle and others and documentaries on the dramatic experiment in criminal redemption which took place in the Barlinnie Special Unit have been the target of the head-in-the-sand brigade. The let's-pretend-it-didn't-happen tendency peaked in 1951 when there was even a move to change the name of the Gorbals ward to "Laurieston". As if changing the name, albeit to an old one for the district, would change history. It failed.

It is gratifying to note that rather than denying the city's criminal history, comedians (and Glasgow has some of the best in the world, many of whom find their stage and audience in a public bar) turn it to good effect. Jokes about getting no glass bottom boats on the Clyde in case you see the bodies play well, even with home audiences. But the city's history of denial is remarkable. One of the most famous books on Glasgow, *The Second City*, first published in 1946, is patronisingly dismissive of McArthur's *No Mean City* and crime writing generally.

Charles Oakley's book is admirable in most respects – the title reflecting the heady days when Glasgow was indeed the second city of the Empire. It is, however, oddly reluctant to face the facts that grinding poverty, unemployment and a general hopelessness of certain sections of the community can result in gangs, extortion, religious warfare, and now in massive drug misuse.

Oakley makes much of the fact that for a hundred years or so Glasgow was regarded as a place of fairly radical political views. After 1919 it was seen as a city of the far left: the imprint of the Red Clydesiders was worldwide. This was an "embarrassment" that drove away business and investment that would help ameliorate the very conditions that caused many of the problems. The same sort of thinking was transferred to the reporting of crime. Indeed the BBC, and other national news media, was reviled by some Glasgow politicians for highlighting what was going on in the underworld rather than feeding the world a constant stream of "good news". The Scottish ability to carry a Guinness Book of Records sized chip on both shoulders at the same time meant that, although all big cities have the same problems to a degree, highlighting the Glasgow experience was somehow unfair.

Oakley says that the city's tough reputation meant that in many minds abroad it was associated with Chicago, Marseilles or Barcelona. In his opinion these cities with their undoubted overcrowded slums and ghettoes might well be just as undeserving of the tag "tough" as Glasgow. It is a point of view, but one that might not be shared by the men and women who police the streets in all such cities.

To illustrate the light in which the city was viewed in some parts of the world, Oakley tells the story of a Buenos Aires business man trembling in London's Euston Station at the thought of being sent to Glasgow. He was, of course, not met on arrival in Central

15

Station by a thug with an open razor ready with the once popular line "If your ma's no' doing anything tonight get her to stitch this up." But, it has to be admitted, it really could have been different if the South American entrepreneur had taken a stroll after midnight in certain parts of town.

Poor McArthur, whose novel was much misunderstood, got it in the neck from Oakley. He dismissed it as "a sordid book which in spite of (or perhaps because of) its unpleasantness had a considerable circulation".

The chip on the shoulder about media coverage also emerges here in a novel form. And it is something that a veteran newspaper man like myself can't quite dismiss. Charles Oakley had a theory that so many Scots journalists had migrated to Fleet Street that they handpicked the bad news coming out of Scotland to feature in the English press because that was "news" to them.

McArthur and *No Mean City* was also a *bête noir* of Pat Lally, who rose from a Gorbals childhood to be a controversial Lord Provost and who was always agin the picture of the Gorbals as painted by McArthur in the novel. To Lally it was a distorted work of fiction.

It was a popular ploy of newspaper feature editors to send reporters into the Gorbals to find people still alive with memories of the days when McArthur's fictional Johnny Stark swaggered the streets with his fearsome razor. Almost to a man or woman they found folk who said that, exaggerated as it was, *No Mean City* was far from off the mark.

And there is no denying that just before the Second World War an investigation into gangsters in the city was halted by a more pressing problem posed by a former house painter from Austria. The Glasgow gangs were, and are, no fictional invention.

But the current battles are far removed from the days of the Billy Boys and the Norman Conks or indeed the immediate post-Second World War gangs. It is revealing to recall that when Walter Norval, said to be the first Godfather of crime in the city, appeared in court accused of being concerned in the supply of amphetamine in 1999 when he was aged seventy-one, he stated his abhorrence of the drug trade and his embarrassment about the suggestion that he was connected with it. He admitted having cannabis worth £15 in his possession – he found it helpful to treat the pain of his arthritis – and was found not guilty of being concerned in the supply of drugs. The court was told that the OAP, who had hobbled into the dock, was helping on a voluntary basis with a drug rehabilitation programme in the city.

In Norval's day as a crime capo, armed robbery and carefully planned hits on hospital payrolls and banks were what gangsterism was all about. The early career of Norval's successor as Godfather, Arthur Thompson Snr, was noted for extortion, money lending and robbery rather than drugs.

The change, when it came, was part of a worldwide trend. An expert on the Mafia in Italy points out that up until the mid-seventies there were only a handful of drug-related deaths, mostly heroin, in Trapani province. This Mafia heartland was up till then mainly noted for the protection racket, vastly expensive bogus public works that produced sections of motorway that led nowhere and overpasses used by the occasional sheep. All of that was a gold mine for the gangsters, but the growth of drug-taking was an opportunity not to be scorned. Within a few years the heroin epidemic was claiming hundreds of lives and several hundred thousands were said to be addicted. All this was producing millions for the men in control of the operation which saw drugs from Turkey flood into Italy.

Much the same was happening in America where most of the Mafia money had previously been raised by extortion, gambling, prostitution and building scams.

The old ways of Glasgow hard men began to change as well. Young Arthur Thompson, aka Fat Boy or the Mars Bar Kid, tried unsuccessfully to step into the big boots of his legendary gangster father. And he was quickly into the drug business, the new string in the bow for the get-rich-quick merchants.

The war for control of the drugs business exploded on the

streets of Glasgow. In March 1992 Paul Ferris, then as now baby faced, and with the appearance of a successful young business man, stood trial accused of seven charges:

1. The supply of heroin, cocaine, and ecstasy.
2. Attempting to murder Arthur Thompson Snr by repeatedly driving a motor car at him in May 1990.
3. Conspiring to assault John "Jonah" McKenzie on 26 May 1991.
4. Shooting William Gillen in the legs and threatening to murder him.
5. Murdering Arthur Thompson Jnr in 1991 while acting with Robert Glover and Joseph Hanlon.
6. Illegal possession of a firearm.
7. Breach of the Bail Act.

Defended by Donald Findlay Q.C., Paul Ferris was found not guilty on all charges and walked free after a sensational trial.

The background to the trial was a full scale turf war in the city with several factions fighting for control of the lucrative drug trade.

Despite his fearsome reputation, power and high visibility, and being at the heart of much of the criminality in the east end for many years, Arthur Snr only spent relatively short times behind bars. And his convictions were fairly minor.

He lived in a well protected home that was virtually a fort, close to Hogganfield Loch. This fortress, known to all and sundry in the city as the Ponderosa, was for a time home to young Arthur, though his efforts to keep up with big boys in the drug trade soon found him going north to the menacing precincts of Peterhead prison where he began an 11-year sentence for drug dealing.

His removal from the scene coupled with his father's "retirement" sowed the seeds of a struggle for control of drugs in the city which resonates to this day. With Ferris later removed for a number of years for gun running, the wars eased and the newspapers spent more time reporting ballet than Berettas.

But the release of Ferris lit a short blue touch paper and upset the way the drugs trade operated in Glasgow in the late nineties. Various "teams" ran the business, each in control of a lucrative area with the biggest concentration of users, and dealers, in the east end and the north, mainly Maryhill (and Possilpark) and Springburn.

Ferris's reappearance had set the blood flowing on the streets yet again. And despite the whitewash merchants there will be more to come. And no doubt more rows about the reporting of it. Anyone who has had anything to do with the recording of crime in Glasgow has ready experience of the pressure to play down or ignore much of what happens.

Back in the 1970s there was a classic example. The BBC sent a television team up from London to examine gangs and brutality in a city which had, at the time, a murder rate on a par with Northern Ireland. When the programme was aired, showing young gang members producing swords and hatchets for the cameras, a classic Glasgow stushie between politicians and the media began. Apparently no fee had been mentioned to the youngsters who showed their weapons with sickening pride. But after the film was in the can the BBC tipped the lads a fiver to be split eight ways, this being what television calls a "field" payment. The practice is not unusual and often small payments are made to extras used on location.

But when news of the money leaked out, the TV folk were accused of setting up film to disgrace a friendly city. It was, according to some, a media conspiracy, something that was always happening to poor old Glasgow. Shades of Charles Oakley.

The distinguished political analyst Murray Ritchie, writing in the then *Glasgow Herald*, trenchantly got to the heart of the matter, just one of many similar rows. He wrote: "Glasgow is a violent, vandalised slum city. That is a fact. But to say so nowadays is, it appears, to be guilty of heresy.

"The BBC programme Nationwide have become the latest

heretic. Their sin was to contravene the unwritten, but apparently inviolable, law which has become established in the past few years. It may not even be a law: more a state of mind.

"The City Chambers promote it, the police support it, and the establishment in general abides by it. Simply interpreted it is this: 'Thou shalt not tell the truth about Glasgow'. And its existence betrays a rather worrying reluctance by some to come to terms with reality."

He went on to point out that Glasgow's problems – a particularly potent mixture in the seventies of crime, alcohol abuse and genuine squalor – are matters of public interest and concern and the reporting of them is in the public interest. They cannot be ignored or swept under the municipal carpet.

Much has changed since this powerful piece of journalism was written. And many of the changes for the better in this great city are a result of facing facts, and doing something about it, not hiding from them.

Historian John Prebble once called Glasgow a "bold and defiant city" and said its "brawling, questioning people" are its majesty.

But for some of the citizens of the Dear Green Place the brawling is in the blood. Not to recognise that is quite simply unrealistic. And counter-productive.

2

CUT AFF ANE LUG!

Like it or not the image of Glasgow as the home of the razor slasher is indelibly printed on the minds of millions. But today the glint of the open razor on the street has virtually disappeared to be replaced by more sophisticated, but equally damaging weapons.

And the open razor itself has dropped into history, even in its original role as an aid to grooming, replaced by the electric razor or the three-bladed safety razor, toiletry accessories unlikely to threaten anyone. But the Glasgow razor slasher is no myth, no fantasy dreamed up by a media plotting to blacken the name of the city. It was a reality and many a citizen walked in fear of attack. Many and varied were the weapons of the street fighter and that will be dealt with later in this book. But for a gangster in the bad old days the cut throat razor had unique attractions. One was its ability to be hidden up a sleeve, light but lethal it was a perfect weapon to scar an enemy, or wielded at the neck it had the ability to kill. In the history of the Glasgow police it is recorded that at one stage constables wore a sort of leather collar as protection against a razor slasher attacking from the back. The advent of the original safety razor with its single removable blade didn't ameliorate the problem. Such a blade was easily hidden in a cap rim, or a handbag, or even set into a stick or pole to manufacture a wicked and fearsome weapon.

So prolific is the legend of the Glasgow razor slasher it is remarkable that there is so little photographic evidence of it in use. But one sickening photograph of what it really meant can be seen on the cover of an early eighties book on Glasgow crime by a well-kent city reporter George Forbes who penned his epic, called *Such Bad Company*, with the assistance of Paddy Meehan. Meehan is, of course, the man who served long years in Peterhead, many of them in solitary confinement, for a murder he didn't commit. Only the sterling work of a committee that included Glasgow lawyer Joe "The Great Defender" Beltrami and Ludovic Kennedy, who has made a habit of pleading for the unjustly jailed, got him freed and cleared.

In his latter years Meehan took much to the company of journalists, enjoying a dram with them in their favoured watering holes. When the *Herald* was billeted in the old Rennie Mackintosh building in Mitchell Street the ex-con turned security expert was a regular in the office, enjoying the company of reporters who had, in some cases, highlighted the injustice brought on him by false accusations.

Joe Beltrami dealt with the Meehan case in his book *A Deadly Innocence* but Paddy did not like the famous lawyer's version one bit. And by now he was something of a wordsmith as well as a safebreaker – thanks to many articles in which he cooperated with reporters to tell the inside story.

So he wrote his own story called *Framed by MI5*, a bizarre piece of work filled with unlikely theories, and hawked it on the streets of Glasgow when bookshops wouldn't risk selling his observations. It fell a little short of being a literary triumph, but Paddy had many a story to tell apart from his own and it is no surprise that this interesting man got together with the legendary reporter, George Forbes, to produce a remarkable tale of crime in Glasgow. The cover image is unforgettable. *Scotsman* photographer Alan Milligan was on the spot in Sauchiehall Street to capture the moment of terror with a thug actually in the act of slashing. In the background ordinary hard-working folk are seen going about their business unaware of the horror a few feet away. This was, for the villain, the attraction of an open razor . . . light, easily hidden, and able to be used when least expected.

But not all razor slashers were gang members. A classic case of the lone wolf was Patrick Carracher who ended his days being dragged screaming to the gallows in Barlinnie. He had a long history of assault with knifes and razors and was clearly a psychopath. To cross him on even a minor matter was to risk the flick of a cut-throat razor across the jugular vein. He had already killed but escaped with a jail sentence when in 1945 he finally was convicted of murder and sentenced to hang. His defence fell mainly on the claim that he was a medical psychopath and that the verdict should be that he was of diminished responsibility at the time of the murder. This was a fairly new plea for that day and age and it didn't wash. But despite seemingly having no conception of right and wrong Carracher was no gangster; he was a described as a human time-bomb who created enough mayhem on his own. He, and his razor, just didn't fit into the gang ethos. Many others who carried razors were also outwith the gang culture.

When it came to weapons the thugs could move with the times. The cut-throat was not the only kind of razor to do damage to the faces of the citizenry. One remarkable character in the story of Glasgow gangsters is a man called Bill Gilvear. His memory of weaponry in the gangs is chilling. Growing up in poverty in the Gallowgate he ran with the gangs as a youth. But salvation came with a visit to the famous Tent Hall, just off Gallowgate. He was converted by the evangelist Seth Sykes and devoted many years to spreading Christianity. He was even a counsellor during Billy Graham's famous 1955 crusade in the city.

Bill Gilvear's background as a fourteen-year-old member of the Stick-it gang was a passport to respect when he tried to convert his sometime associates and youngsters who had gone off the rails. In 1991 he was interviewed and described by the reporter as a gentle figure in sports jacket and pebble glasses. But the old memories were still strong. He reached inside his jacket pocket and told the writer: "This is where you kept your bicycle chain hidden. You pulled it out and a member of a rival gang got it against his face. And you took a safety razor and split it in two and that gave you a long thin blade. You hid it in the edge of your cap and if someone said good evening to you, you could slit their throat from ear to ear. We were the terror of the east side of Glasgow."

Newspaper reports down the years have made much of the ingenuity involved in the lethal weapons carried by street fighters. The gangsters excuse – much used in court – was often that they expected to be attacked. This was undoubtedly true. A gang member on his own and well off his turf was always in danger of attack by rivals who recognised him.

The list of weapons is horrific . . . hammers, hatchets, bayonets, sticks filled with lead, huge metal bolts attached to waxed cord and used like an Argentinian bolas, razors of all sorts, broken bottles, shotguns (homemade and stolen), revolvers, swords. The bicycle chain was a favourite, weighty enough to do massive damage when swung violently. A refinement was shown in one fifties gang series in the newspapers – a bicycle chain with the addition of sharp slivers of metal on one end. If all this was not enough a well swung boot (preferably with steel toe caps) came into play when your opponent was downed. Lead coshes and knuckledusters found favour with some. Makeshift weapons were fashioned out of scrap metal. Lengths of heavy chain had spikes welded on. Even swords which were something of a feature in the gang battles of the twenties and thirties were reported to be still carried by thugs after the Second World War. One young "Mod", in the days of regular clashes between "Mods" and "Rockers", was said to drive around Glasgow on his trendy Italian scooter with a sword hidden down his trouser legs.

All this makes it more than somewhat ironic that what was perhaps the first recorded "slashing" in the city was the work of the authorities!

In 1599 one George Mitchell "apprehendit for thift" was warned that if he was caught at it again in the city "ane lug would be cut out of his heid". Not with an open razor one presumes.

Around this time the punishment of mutilation by cutting off an ear was not uncommon. In England there was an even more sophisticated version of the punishment. In some cases of petty theft the offender was nailed to a post by the ear and left there with "a knyffe in hand". This poor wretch might choose the time of his own liberation, but he could only do it by cutting off his ear.

The same document that tells such bloodthirsty tales of justice also makes clear that even around 500 years ago the Mafia/gangland concept of showing respect was strong.

George Mitchell's itchy fingers caused him grief but in the case of "one William Watson alias Blackhouse William" the problem was more cerebral. He stood accused of making disdainful speeches about the authorities and he would not take off his bonnet to the baillie. This was considered to be proud contempt and an "evil example for others to do the like". Thrown into jail, unable to pay his ten pound fine, he threatened to set fire to the jail and protested that "he wad neither acknowledge provost, nor baillie, king nor casart".

This was tough, rebellious talking that could not be tolerated and Blackhouse William found himself back in jail and ordered to walk "bare heidit" to the cross on mercat day, was put in irons for four hours and told to get down on his knees to ask God for mercy and the baillies' pardon. Show respect!

The concept of gangs was still hundreds of years into the future, but there was still much violence on the streets to come before organised crime began to emerge. Most of it came from mobs which have a long history in Glasgow, a city where down the years no one has seemed particularly amenable to authority. Blackhouse Willie has his counterparts in the city's pubs to this day.

And if the gangs were to be a time coming, extortion wasn't. One archive document tells of the abused power of the magistrates in the late seventeenth century. A council minute records "the great clamour made by the townspeople about the abuses committed by magistrates these few years past". The abuses appeared to be imposing fines without any formal court procedures and trousering the proceeds. So specific were these claims that it was decided that "in tyme cuming none of the magistrates within the burgh, baillie of Gorbals or water baillie shall have the power to fine any persone except by conveining the transgressors in a public court".

One of the earliest books on Glasgow – *Old Glasgow, the Place and the People* – was written by Andrew McGeorge and published in 1880. It gives an illuminating view of justice in the late eighteenth century, commentating that the magistrates of Glasgow, "like some of the rulers in Scripture times", were in the habit of standing in the street around Glasgow Cross to hear the suits of the citizens and dispense summary justice.

This is the sort of idea that would no doubt appeal to many a modern policeman or woman weighted down with paperwork, the fear that witnesses would alter their stories in court and aware of juries with a tendency to give the benefit of the doubt to the accused who may live not too far away from a relative or two!

Glasgow Cross and Glasgow Green, not surprisingly, feature strongly in the history of violence in the city. In the twenties and thirties there were pitched battles between rival gangs on the bridges over the Clyde at Glasgow Green. But even that was small beer compared with the Bread Riot in 1848 which was the largest example of mass violence in the city's history. Many of those involved were displaced Highlanders or Irish immigrants, mostly starving and out of work. This famous riot was part of unrest that had been festering throughout Britain since the Reform Act of 1832.

The spirit of the times spawned the Chartist movement to fight social injustice. Early in 1848 there had been revolutionary activity in France and this encouraged the Chartists to hold a meeting on the Green. It is reported that more than 3,000 people turned up for the event which soon became ugly and violent. After the speechifying, rioters went on the rampage looking for weapons and in their fury tore up iron railing in Monteith Row. Next came a march into the city proper and shops were looted, some of the marchers having success, by their standards, with a break-in at a gunsmith's in Royal Exchange Square.

Seemingly they then swarmed into nearby Buchanan Street,

firing their weapons into the air, like extras in a cowboy film. This had an unusual outcome in that a doctor who apparently took the view that guns might be acceptable in Gallowgate, but were not in order in douce Buchanan Street promptly partly disarmed the rioters.

Contemporary reports indicate that the early police force and the town guard had little effect on the mob, and despite the good doctor's efforts, shots were fired into the crowd and several people died. Eventually special constables forced the mob back towards the Gallowgate and the east end. But there was a further twenty-four hours of destruction and mobbing before the army managed to disperse the crowds. Surprisingly there were only around thirty arrests though some of the rioters were sentenced to transportation to Australia.

The Bread Riots may have been the largest and best known, but Glasgow had seen something similar before. More than a hundred years before, in 1727, the Government courted trouble with a plan to impose a tax of sixpence on every barrel of beer brewed. The revenues from Scotland were seen as inadequate and this was to be the solution. Acknowledgment even in these far off days of the Scottish liking for a beer. Public outcry was such that the Government made what in modern parlance would be called a U-turn and cut the proposed tax by half to threepence. It is always, it seems, politically unwise to impose huge tax increases on booze! The Jacobites were described at the time as being in a state of "thinly veiled rebellion" and took every chance of annoying the Government "by tumults and petty raids!"

Enter six troops of Dragoons and Highlanders to restore order in Glasgow. Around this time punishment for rioting was hard. It is recorded that although a man and a woman were liberated, others were sentenced to "perpetual banishment" and others whipped through the streets. The eighteenth century was a time of cruel punishments for relatively trivial offences, including mutilation and flogging. Banishment, too, was a serious matter. According to the "annals of Hawick", a husband and wife convicted of theft were "banished furth of the town under penalty of one year's imprisonment if they return and to be scourged every month during said year and banished under penalty". To be banished "furth of Scotland" meant that the criminal was in effect an outlaw and liable to be hunted down by anyone who recognised him. There was, in modern parlance, no hiding place. You could not simply lie low in another town taking work to keep body and soul together. The rules of the day were such that Kirk Sessions would not allow anyone to reside in the parish unless they could produce a certificate from the Session of his former district. And no farmer could give a wretch bent on rehabilitation a job because of a law passed in 1704 forbidding the employment of any person not holding the all-important certificate. Food for thought in these days when many call for the reintroduction of identity cards. In reality the only course open to the banished was to continue a life of crime with the inevitable consequence of ending up back in court. Anyone reckless enough to return to their place of conviction was promptly scourged or branded. Sometimes he would be held in jail subject to payment of £100 Scots – a sum far too high for a peasant to pay for his freedom.

The punishment of banishment lingered on until the latter half of the eighteenth century, when the growth of large towns made it easier for the wrongdoer to conceal himself. Only then did the sentence "furth of Scotland" fall into disuse. One of the last recorded cases of this cruel and iniquitous punishment occurred in 1755 when James M'Arthur and his wife Jean were brought before the Gorbals' bailies charged with being proprietors of a disorderly house. Witnesses called by James Maxwell, procurator fiscal of the Barony and Justiciary of Gorbals, were examined and the magistrates found the offence proved and "adjudged and decerned the defenders to be carried from the bar to the common prison in the chapel of the Gorbals and there to be detained until the sixteenth day of September current, at 12 o'clock on which day ordained, and hereby ordain that the defenders be carried from the said prison, and by tuck of drum, with their heads bare and uncovered, to be banished and hereby banish them from the village and Barony of the Gorbals during the whole of their natural lives; with certification to them that if they, or either of them, shall after their banishment aforesaid, return or be found in the said village or barony, they shall be apprehended and imprisoned in prison aforesaid and publicly whipped through the said village of Gorbals on the first Wednesday after their imprisonment; and so often as the offenders return, or be found in the said village during the space of this banishment and hereby grant warrant for apprehending, imprisoning, whipping and banishment of them."

All this was happening at a time when the magistrates of Glasgow had almost abandoned the old penalty and reformers were fighting for banishment to be completely removed as a punishment. The legality of the sentence on the M'Arthurs was questioned on the grounds that although the magistrates of Glasgow might enjoy the right of exiling criminals on the strength of their city being a royal burgh, the same did not apply to the Gorbals which ranked only as a burgh or barony. There was earlier evidence in favour of this line of thought in an Act of Parliament in 1748 repealing heritable jurisdictions in Scotland. And even earlier when the Barony of Gorbals was transferred to the City of Glasgow by Sir Robert Douglas in 1647, a special Bill was passed through the Scottish Parliament confirming to the Glasgow magistrates "All and hail the six pound land of old extent of Gorbals and Bridge-end with the heritable office of bailiary and Justiciary within the said bounds".

It seems that the Gorbals bailies were in future content to accept this proof that in serious cases their jurisdiction must bow before that of Glasgow. After the banishment of the M'Arthurs no more criminals were sent "furth of Scotland" and instead were jailed or fined. Incidentally, around this time the stocks were still in use for minor crime though the delinquent was forced to spend only three hours at a time, in daylight, in this cruel and shaming form of punishment. The M'Arthur incident was indicative of a major change in society and a rethink with the prevention of crime coming to the forefront of the public mind as well as the reform of cruel punishments.

All this was a major wake-up call about the potential for crime and violence brought about by poverty and unemployment. And the need for a well organised police authority to tackle crime.

The city, however, was well ahead of its time in policing. The popular misconception is that Robert Peel in London in 1828 was the man behind modern policing. But, in fact, Glasgow was away ahead of the game. The city's police force has roots that go back to the Glasgow Police Act of 1800. This precedes by twenty-nine years the date when Robert Peel started an organised force. So Glasgow it seems deserves a higher place in the history of law and order than it is normally accorded. But the need for proper organised law enforcement in the city was recognised even before 1800, in 1788 when those magistrates – so criticised in the past – began to look at community policing. Up till then the job of keeping the villains under control was tackled by a combination of watchmen and the city guard which was made up of ordinary townspeople.

This early attempt at building a police force didn't last. The money ran out and it took an Act of Parliament to solve the problem. Early minutes show that in 1789 a Master of Police was appointed. Being chief of police in Glasgow is never going to be easy but the first boss had the handicap of having a mere eight constables working with him to keep the streets and businesses safe.

By 1800 the Glasgow Police Force was officially formed and had its first headquarters in the session house of the Laigh Kirk in Trongate. The entire annual cost of the operation would barely buy petrol for a year for a squad car today – £2,676. The master of police was paid £200, clerk £85, treasurer £80, three sergeants at £40 each, nine day officers at £30 each, sixty-eight watchmen at £26 each and boxes for night watchmen cost £153.

History tells us that the immediate effect of forming a regular force was to drive thieves and rogues of all sorts from the city into surrounding areas which all then had to think of a police force of their own. The watchmen, as they tended to be called, wore greatcoats with an identification number painted on the back. Originally each watchman was given a sentry box to shelter from the weather when necessary, which was then, as now, frequently. The boxes filled this role so well that on occasion, again then as now a cynic might say, you could not find a policeman – they were all sheltering in their boxes leaving the city to look after itself. Soon regulations were introduced limiting the number of coppers who could shelter in their boxes at any given time. The sentry boxes had a disadvantage that was quickly discovered by the ever inventive Glasgow ned. If you tipped one over from behind, with a policeman inside it, he could not get out unless helped by a colleague. Trapping the lawmen in their boxes became quite a game for a time. A ploy with a humorous side, but a tad more serious than a Woosterish passion for knocking off policemen's hats when squiffy. It was a police force very different from that of today – the early officers even had responsibility for sweeping the streets.

Huge changes in operation, technology and police numbers (the first force was eighty-three-strong) came to the modern city with a succession of remarkably successful chief constables, with Sir Percy Sillitoe best remembered as the man who invented many of the modern techniques of crime control and as a legend who, for a time, brought the gangs of the thirties to heel with a violent approach that would today bring howls of protest from the politically correct. Perhaps his best known successor is Sir David McNee who also led the Met. in London. Many others did battle with the gangs of their era – Sir James Robertson and Sir Andrew Sloan, Sir Leslie Sharp and Sir John Orr among them. All became household names in a city where the newspapers report the doings of the gangs – and their changes in leadership and personnel – with missionary zeal that is perhaps based on the ability of a good crime exclusive to boost circulation.

Many more than the eight constables of yore are required to

keep the peace in modern Glasgow. At the time of writing the latest figures show a force of 7,200 (down on the notional figure of 7,352). The average age of a constable is thirty-seven with thirteen years of service, so the force is an experienced one. Interestingly, fifty-five officers were performing seconded duties with the Scottish Drug Enforcement Agency.

The current force presides over a murder rate (including culpable homicide at common law) that has declined from eighty-five in 1999/2000 to sixty-five in 2000/2001. Statistics also show that carrying offensive weapons and possession of firearms with intent to injure or commit crime rose slightly, while the carrying of knives or blades fell marginally. But nonetheless crime related to carrying offensive weapons and knives remained close to a high in the trend for the last ten years. Most drug offences, from cultivation to supply and possession, showed rises.

But almost before the ink on the report was dry, stories emerged in the newspapers, as they tend to do in Glasgow, that perhaps the police were hamstrung in their attempts to control the crime figures – especially with regard to the under 16s. Young teens play a major part in the new street battles between gangs and are particularly involved in the horrifying trend of attacking fire crews on the way to or from, or even at, an incident.

The emergency services have to consider the possibility that a 999 call could be setting them up for an attack. Some Tory politicians and police officers think much of the blame lies with the children's panel system. Set up in 1968 the idea is to separate children who commit crimes from those who require care and protection. Few could argue with the concept. A double whammy of a shortage of lay people willing to sit on the panels and a shortage of social workers is handicapping the scheme in 2002. One report claimed that at a time when there were 2,400 children on supervision orders in the city, up to 700 had no social worker. There are complaints of too much bureaucracy and that the system instils little fear in hardened young neds. There were many who harked back to the days when a possible court appearance before an old fashioned sheriff could deter a young thug.

The police, too, have their complaints about the system. The *Evening Times*, which always keeps a close and perceptive eye on matters criminal in the city, had an insightful interview with Norrie Flowers, chairman of the Scottish Police Federation, which represents rank and file officers. In his view more resources for the police could help arrest more young offenders but do little to stem the tide of youth crime. He said: "There are so many excellent aspects to the children's panel system that it would be wrong to rubbish it. But it just can't deal with repeat offenders, the hardened neds who while fewer in number than people might think, do create a lot of havoc.

"The police know these people. They can arrest them as many times as they want, but before the ink is dry on the police report they are back on the streets. Perhaps what we need is to put these hardened youngsters in front of a real court with real punishments so they can realise the severity of what they've done."

These sentiments were echoed by Cardonald councillor Alistair Watson, a former magistrate, whose area is badly affected by warring gangs of youngsters. In his view the idea of getting the general public to play a role in dispensing justice is good. But he argues that the public themselves don't see it working as a deterrent. He told the *Evening Times*: "I am friendly with people who sit on the children's panel and they are exasperated with the system. And the police know they are powerless when it comes to dealing with the same offenders over and over again.

"This is not to mention dragging policemen from their shifts to give evidence in cases which don't sit and burning police hours with their reports which may never be used. The criminal justice system need to be radically overhauled with something that works."

Jon Bannister, a youth crime expert at Glasgow University, took a slightly more sanguine view in this debate. In his view most youngsters will eventually grow out of crime. But in the short term he was of the opinion that although the children's panel system has merits, some of the fundamental principles had been forgotten. "What appears wrong in Scotland is that there is difficulty finding a balance between preventing crime and managing crime. There are problems with the children's panels and there are problems in certain areas with young criminals. But whether it is any worse now than in previous eras is open to question."

But Tory MSP Bill Aitken was forceful. "The police don't have enough teeth and the children's panel is impotent. The criminal justice system needs to introduce more punative measures for young people such as weekend detentions and community service. As for attacks on fire crews, who are often on their way to save lives and property, I believe the only punishment is a custodial sentence."

The debate on how to deal with crime, and not just the teenage gangs but the whole business of drug gangs, turf warfare and the control of prostitution and extortion, threads its way through the entire story of crime in the city.

We may have moved a long way from "cutting aff ane lug", and the sickening ritual of capital punishment is now a memory in a city where the hangman often found work. But his activities certainly attracted much public attention, with more than 80,000 people turning out to see the last public hanging in Glasgow. The last man put to death with an audience was the infamous poisoner Dr Edward Pritchard in 1865.

The legendary Glasgow journalist Jack House deals with the case at great length in his famous book *Square Mile of Murder*, republished this year, and describes the doctor's final minutes as reported in the newspapers of the time: "When he appeared on the scaffold great commotion prevailed among the crowd. Exclamations were heard to proceed from every quarter, among which were such expressions as 'how well he looks', 'he's very pale', 'that's him' and 'hats off'. A short prayer was read while the hangman Calcraft adjusted the cap, put aside the long hair and beard to allow the rope to be rightly placed and tied the legs.

"Calcraft, after putting the rope around the prisoner's neck, and drawing the cap over his face, steadied the wretched man by placing his hands on his back and breast. On a signal being given by the culprit the bolt was drawn and at ten minutes past eight he was launched into eternity. As soon as he was seen dangling from the rope a loud shriek was heard from the crowd and many turned their heads away from the horrid spectacle."

A grisly interest was to continue however with public hunger for news of executions, crowds outside prison gates at the appointed hour and a black flag flying from the prison flagpole. There has been continued fascination down the years with the loathsome Dr Pritchard who even had the coffin lid unscrewed so that he could kiss the dead lips of the wife he had tortured by slow poisoning.

A splendid Glasgow institution was the waxworks and Pritchard was for years the prime exhibit in the shows run by eccentric Glasgow showman A. E. Pickard who also ran some of the earliest city cinemas. One of Pickard's most popular attractions was a "working model" of the execution of a murderer. And whenever a new murderer was hanged in Glasgow – a fairly frequent occurrence – the waxworks staff would change the clothes of the dummy in the model and label it with the name of the new murderer. Thus it was said that the model, if gruesome, was at least up to date.

Age was no barrier in the heyday of the rope. After the gallows in Glasgow Green went out of favour, Duke Street Prison was the place of death for many a villain. What death by hanging was really like is illustrated in the newspaper accounts of the 1925 execution of John Keen for killing an Indian pedlar in a house in Port Dundas. The right for women over thirty to vote was won in 1918 (it was to be 1929 before the legal limit was dropped to twenty-one) but women were already making inroads into public life and the despatch of Keen was the first execution in Glasgow to be witnessed by a woman magistrate, called upon to exercise the grim realities of public life. Keen, it was reported, showed great fortitude and walked with firm step and erect figure to the scaffold. Pierpoint was the hangman. Bailie Mrs Bell was a junior magistrate and one of an official party that included another magistrate, Dr James Dunlop, the prison governor, the chief constable and the town clerk depute. A large crowd had gathered in Cathedral Square and it loitered around for some time before and after the hanging which took place at the traditional hour of 8 a.m. The papers reported that Mrs Bell went through the ordeal "unflinchingly and retained full self-possession through this trying experience". She was said to be pale but quite composed when she emerged from the prison after the execution. Interviewed later at her home she said she had not been in the least upset or nervous at the ordeal, adding that there was really nothing in the proceedings to upset any woman possessed of ordinary nerves. Keen was calm and collected when she saw him in the cells. Immediately after he had replied to the question of his identity the murderer asked the magistrates "will you shake hands with me?" Both bailies agreed to the request and Mrs Bell said the act seemed to afford him some immediate comfort. After this the official party was taken to the place of execution and had just taken up their positions when Keen arrived. "He was pale but carried his head high and went unhesitatingly to his place. There was no scene of any kind." He was dead forty-five seconds after leaving his cell.

The press raised the question of the fitness of a woman to undertake such an onerous duty. Mrs Bell, who seems by all accounts to have been a remarkable woman, said that she felt that when a woman offered herself as a member of the town council she should be prepared to take up all the duties which appertained to the office of bailie or magistrate. She was convinced that any of the woman members of Glasgow corporation could have equally well undertaken the duty. In the afternoon of the execution a formal inquiry was held under a sheriff in the County Buildings when witnesses confirmed what had gone on and the prison doctor Gilbert Gerry confirmed that he had examined the body "and found life to be extinct". A grim ritual indeed.

Interestingly the first person to be hanged in the new prison of

Barlinnie, John Lyon, was barely out of his teens when he took the last few fateful steps to the gallows. And the last was even younger, nineteen-year-old Tony Miller, labelled by the press as the "boy killer". He died just three days before Christmas 1960 for his part in the killing of a homosexual in a park in the south side of the city. Revulsion against the death penalty was growing and around 30,000 people petitioned the then Scottish Secretary, John S. McLay, for leniency. Justice however took its cold course.

The arguments about the death penalty, its deterrent value and the morality of society killing in the public name continue to this day. But long throw-away-the-key sentences are another matter.

Ten or so years earlier than Miller's hanging had seen the most remarkable curbing of the razor slashers and gangsters. This was a time of one of the seemingly regular recurring peaks of gang crime in the city. Then a fearsome figure on the bench, Lord Carmont, moved in on the scene. He had one key thought – those guilty of slashing or other acts of violence should be locked away for long periods. This theory he applied with consistency and success. Indeed being sent down for a long stretch became known among the thugs on the streets of Glasgow as "copping a Carmont". Somewhat ironically the judge himself was a man with a fine sense of humour, recognised as a kindly gentle man away from the court.

But his sentences worked. The *Herald* said of him: "His salutary sentences on razor-slashers, knife-wielders and thugs in the Glasgow High Court in the years following the Second World War had a marked effect on the criminal classes and earned for him the respect and approval of law-abiding citizens." In one circuit the hard man judge imposed sentences of up to ten years and a total of 52 years' imprisonment on eight people convicted of "crimes of violence". One thing is for sure: the debate on how to deal with the gangsterism (which is still with us after all these years and all the different policies of dealing with it, from iron hand to velvet glove) will go on.

3

WHAT'S IN A NAME?

Graffiti is a fact of modern life. There is hardly a city in the world where the spray-gun merchants have not made their mark. And with the occasional exception of street-sharp wit or misguided artistic talent it is something that most people can live without. For a Glaswegian it is sad to say that the most vivid memory of graffiti is often of the letters "FTP" scrawled wickedly and provocatively, usually in red, over any available wall or other public space. Especially in areas known to have a sizeable Roman Catholic community. The sectarian divide in the city makes the vicar of Rome a target of hate for some. "FTP" apart, perhaps the most seen piece of graffiti, or the most heard pub aside, was "Tongs ya bass". The original Glasgow Tong gang was apparently spawned in the Calton, though other gangs used the term as in the Milton Tong and the Toon Tong of Townhead. The use of the word tong, you can be sure, did not spring from gangsters' grannies using a genteel piece of fine silver to direct sugar cubes in the direction of a cup of Tommy Lipton's tea. Tongs, in a worldwide concept, are the infamous legendary Chinese protection gangs much featured in cheap paperback literature. In particular they played a role in California and Nevada in the lawless gold rush days. If the Chinese laundry was a staple cliché in turn-of-the-century low-life literature, so too was the fear of the tongs.

But the use of the term in Glasgow is much more recent. In October '68 a group of gang members told a *Daily Telegraph* reporter that they adopted the name for their gang after a visit to the local

38

flea pit to see a film called "Terror of the Tongs". According to the splendid *Halliwell's Film Guide* this was the story of a Hong Kong merchant who avenged the death of his daughter at the hands of a secret society. It is said to be a gory melodrama with dollops of screams, torture and vaguely orgiastic episodes. It certainly hit the spot with the Glasgow thugs. Even as they left the cinema they ran wild, breaking windows and shouting "Tongs ya Bass".

Long before this, in the 1880s, the Penny Mob became the first familiar gang name in the city. This bunch of rogues took their name from their habit of collectively chipping in a penny a week to help pay fines levied on the members for their crimes. Their main area of operation was said to be Townhead and their longevity as a gang was such that it took till the Sillitoe era for them to be destroyed. In early reports in the *Evening Times* in the twenties and thirties it was said, "This gang had a common fund to which all contributed, and when members were fined in the police courts the money was always forthcoming – hence the name 'Penny Mob'. Their picturesque name should not disguise the fact that they were a gang of hooligans who for long were a source of serious annoyance to the community."

An article written by a reporter with close contact with the ringleaders of the Penny Mob contained reminiscences of one member who made it clear that the Mob had many street fights with other gangs.

The boys of the Wee Do'e Hill and the Big Do'e Hill were rivals. There was also a gang styled the Drygate Youths who, on one occasion it was reported, "while holding high revel fell foul of the police and a battle royal ensued. This particular stramash ended with the arrest of an individual described as the 'chairman of the gang.'"

One man who had an interesting association with the Penny Mob was Robert Earle May who left Glasgow for America in the 1880s but never forgot his roots. Indeed he and his wife raised the sizeable sum of $15,000 dollars to erect a statue of Robert Burns in Boston. When he returned to Glasgow on a holiday in the thirties he sought out a reporter to give him his thoughts. He saw much change for good in the city but "found gang and sectarian warfare still flourishing". He showed the reporter an article he had written in an Anglo-American periodical called *The Fiery Cross* containing his personal reminiscences of the days when the Penny Mob harassed certain sections of the city. He told of the street fights with the boys of the "Wee Do'e Hill and the Big Do'e Hill" when the ammunition was broken whin stones from the railway tracks of the New City railway, then being constructed, helped out with paling stobs and wash boiler lids. This was the pre-safety razor era and other weapons were belts and fists. Mr May says that when he was "young and foolish" he had an occasional arrangement with the ringleader of this gang to obtain the services of members as "chuckers-out" at public meetings when the speakers could not be sure of a fair hearing. However the chuckers-out became a bit too enthusiastic and the arrangement was cancelled!

The influence of the cinema in naming gangs such as the Tongs is also evident back during the First World War when the Cowboys and the Redskins made headlines rather different from those that recorded the opening up of the old West.

Glasgow was not alone with its puzzling gang names, like the Bloodhound Flying Corps – Manchester had its Bengal Tigers and Birmingham the Peaky Blinders. The gangs had some ingenuity in choosing names, but sometimes the smaller outfits tried to cash in on the notoriety of the legendary gangs. The Billy Boys of Bridgeton, led by William Fullerton, clearly signalled their Orange connections and you could also find smaller outfits elsewhere in the city styling themselves "Billy Boys".

Less obvious was the choice of The Cody for a Queenslie gang. Some have it that this stood for Come On Die Young, others favoured Cowards Only Die Young.

Irony surfaces with the Choirboys of Scotstoun. As in the Billy Boys, Irish politics surfaces in the Coburg Erin and the Calton Emmet, a name which owes much to folk memory – Emmet being an Irish patriot executed in 1803! A touch of more modern day hero worship is to be seen in names like McGrory Boys and Milligan Boys. Jimmy McGrory was a famous Celtic player and manager and Tommy Milligan a boxer with a huge southside following. Milligan narrowly failed to win the world title, losing out to the great Mickey "Toy Bulldog" Walker in 1927. In his retirement he ran a famous pub in the Gorbals.

Names often followed as the gang members and their families moved out of city centre slums to the new schemes like Castlemilk, Drumchapel and Easterhouse. The idealism that created such massive estates with housing better than that of the old crumbling tenements, with their unsanitary outside toilets and dampness, was praiseworthy in many ways. But the omission of swimming pools, cinemas, libraries, bars and restaurants undoubtedly contributed to creating new areas of crime. Comedian Billy Connolly's description of such schemes as "deserts wae windaes" can raise a laugh from Glaswegians, who whatever their faults can never by any stretch of the imagination be accused of lacking a sense of humour, but it is painfully accurate. At one stage Castlemilk had a larger population than Perth and no public facilities. The gangs which thrived in this environment simply carried the old names with them, hence the Castlemilk Cumbie and the Castlemilk Fleet, tributes in a way to the infamous gangs of the Gorbals.

The Ku Klux Klan was a sort of offshoot of the Billy Boys. Fullerton's men had an unusually well organised structure and while the Glasgow KKK seemed to forswear white hoods and burning crosses, they wore identifying black and white ties and badges with K on them.

In the same way lesser gangs like the Gray Street Billy Boys copied the originals. The Brigton Billy Boys' great rivals, the Norman Conks of Norman St, were mirrored in the Nuneaton Conks of Nuneaton Street.

There was no difficulty in finding something for rival gangs to fight over. The *Evening Citizen* in 1930, in an examination of the gangs, found that girlfriends were as ever a cause of dispute. It thundered that girls accompanying gang members to the picture house or the dancing hall often proved a source of contention. According to the investigator, a fight "over a girl" has been a feature of the human story ever since Menalaos and Paris fought for fair Helen! The conclusion was that the citizens of Glasgow should not, therefore, be alarmed when their young men fight over a girl.

Although some girls did join the gangs, in the early days women seemed to have played a very minor role, relegated to bathing and bandaging the warriors' wounds and visiting them when imprisoned and all the while struggling to bring up their offspring on meagre cash flows.

An exception appears briefly in the newspapers of the time with an intriguingly inadequate reference to The Nudies who apparently had a girl leader called Queen of The Nudies, shades of Lady Godiva. In fact there is speculation that the Godiva legend was behind the naming of the gang. What little that is known about their remarkable leader would not encourage Hollywood or even the newly booming Scottish film industry to make a movie on The Nudies, starring Madonna or Nicole Kidman, though clearly the title would be a sure-fire box office attraction. The leader, called Mary, was said to have a striking face and a strong personality but "was not possessed of much beauty of feature or form". In fact she was very small and bandy-legged (a common Glasgow affliction caused by poor diet). She led her gang in several fights. She was arrested twice and jailed the second time for twenty days. This apparently effectively ended the reign of the twentieth century Scottish Godiva.

Another curiosity to the modern Glaswegian would be the fact that there were apparently at one time two gangs in the George Street/Shuttle Street area – The Lollipops and Joytown, though Joytown are sometimes referred to as coming from the nearby Cathedral/Castle Street area. In the heyday of the gangs George Street was lined with tenements, wine shops and churches in the usual rich Glasgow mixture. Even in the fifties when I worked in nearby Albion Street, old timers could buy cheap jugs of wine from barrels in an attempt to temporarily blot out the misery of such surroundings. But latterly it became something of an urban desert with tax offices, Strathclyde University, the old *Herald* print works and massive car parks, hardly a prime breeding ground for gang warfare. Now, of course, it is on the fringe of the revitalised Merchant City and the most likely source of crime would be a sushi raid or a hit on a purveyor of Asian noodles, such is the preponderance of exotic restaurants in the area.

There is great debate on the effect TV has on crime and an inconclusive war continues to rage between factions who believe that gang films provoke crime and others who regard them as harmless. But some of Glasgow's young neds seemed much influenced by "The Man from Uncle" TV series starring David McCallum. Ruchill had a gang called Uncle and in Townhead they named a gang Thrush, after McCallum's on-screen enemies.

The following list of gang names is not comprehensive. Down the years Glasgow has had hundreds of gangs ranging from the Billy Boys who had up to 800 members, to little groups who simply hung around street corners, like the Blackhill youngsters who failed to stretch their imagination when choosing their name – the Corner Boys.

The origin of some gang names now seems a mystery – like Ging Gong or the Gold Dust Gang. Others have often been the subject of debate in the press. The Baltic Fleet was one of the longest lasting gangs – in operation in some form or other from the thirties till at least the nineties. But there are no exotic maritime connections in the name. The accepted derivation seems to be that the Baltic Jute Company of Dundee had a factory in Baltic Street in Bridgeton which failed quite quickly after an opening flourish. The gang lasted longer and it is interesting to note that in a case mentioning it in the nineties, Edgar Prais Q.C. talked of gang fights in Easterhouse being arranged like "Saturday fixtures".

The derivation of the Billy Boys in a strongly protestant area like Bridgeton is obvious but the more exotic sounding Norman Conks has a fairly mundane explanation. The name often caused speculation in the columns of the *Herald* but seems merely to have come from the Norman Street area and the idea of being a "conqueror".

A

Aggro

Anderston

Antique Mob – Shettleston

Apaches

Argyle Billy Boys – Bridgeton
(Hosier Street)

B

Bal Toi – Easterhouse

Baltic Fleet – Bridgeton

Bar G – Bargeddie

Bar L – Barlanark

Barlanark Team

Bath – Anderston

Beehive – Gorbals

Bell On Boys

Big Do'e Hill

Billy Boys – Bridgeton Cross

Bingo Boys – Govan

Biro Minors – Bridgeton

Bishopbriggs Toi

Bison – Bishopbriggs

Black Diamond Boys – Southside

Black Hand

Black Muffler – Clydebank

Black Star – Calton

Blackhill Toi

* I doubt that any complete list of the names of all Glasgow's gangs can be found or compiled. The names listed here are simply those mentioned in the books, documents, and newspapers consulted in research for this book. Some gangs would be a handful of nasties whose existence would run for a mere few weeks. Sometimes there could be hundreds of members and a gang's malign influence could haunt an area for years or even decades. Sometimes the area of the gang's influence is evident in the name, sometimes gangs ranged across several areas. Indeed the battle for control of turf is one of the main driving forces in gangland and the names reflect that. Many a Glaswegian will have in his memory the name of a gang or two not mentioned in this list – for some gangs managed to exist without being chronicled in the papers or the members even meeting a social worker! Or a policeman!

Blade – Eastfield
Bloodhound Flying Corps
Blue Angels
Border – Tollcross/Parkhead
Bowrie – Whiteinch
Brig Ahoy
Brigade – Bridgegate
Brigton Derry – Bridgeton
Buck – Drumchapel
Bundy – Priesthill
Butny Boys – Maryhill
BYC – Busby Young Cumbie

C
Cadder Young Team
Calton Emmet – Stevenson Street/
    Abercrombie Street
Calton Entry Mob – Tollcross
Castlemilk Cumbie
Castlemilk Fleet
Castlemilk Toi
Castlemilk Young Team
Cheeky Forty – Roystonhill
Choirboys – Scotstoun
Coburg Erin
Coby Heind Team – Ruchazie
Cody – Queenslie
Corner Boys – Blackhill
Cow Toi – Cowcaddens
Cowboys – Dennistoun
Craigton Goucho
Crossy Possie – Govan
Cumbie – Gorbals

D
Dally Boys – Dalmarnock Road
Death Valley Boys
Dempsey Boys – Govan
Den Toi – Easterhouse
Derry Boys – Bridgeton
Dickie – Bridgeton
Diehards – Govan
Dirty Dozen – Southside
Drummie – Easterhouse
Dumbarton Riot Squad
Drygate Youths

E
Easterhouse Derry

F
Fenian Drummy – Drumchapel

G
Gestapo – Dennistoun
Ging Gong
Gold Dust Gang – Gorbals
Goucho – Carntyne
Govan Team
Gray Street Billy Boys
Gringo – Barmulloch
Gyto – Garthamlock

H
Haghill Toi
Hall Boys – Bridgeton
Hammer Boys – Southside
Haugh Boys – Partick
Hazel Boys – Bridgeton

Hi-Hi's – Mile End
Himshie – Cambuslang
Hole-in-the-head
Hutchie – Gorbals/Polmadie

I
ICF – Inter City Firm

J
Joytown – George Street/
    Shuttle Street
Jungo Boys – Possilpark

K
Kelly Bow – Govan
Kelly Boys
Kelly Boys – Govan
Kent Star Boys – Calton
Kill Me Deads
Kinning Park Rebels (KPR)
Kinning Park Star
Ku Klux Klan – Bridgeton

L
Lady Buck – Drumchapel
Liberty Boys – Gorbals
Lollipops – George Street/
    Shuttle Street

M
Mealy Boys – Southside
Milligan Boys – Anderston
Milton Tongs
McGlyn Push – Southside
McGrory Boys – Bridgegate

Monks – Dennistoun
Monty Boys – Mongomery Street,
    Dalmarnock
Mummies

N
Naburn Billies
Norman Conks – Bridgeton
Nudies – Errol Street
Nuneaton Conks –
    Nuneaton Street/Parkhead
Nunnie Boys – Bridgeton

P
Parlour Boys
Peachy Boys – London Road
Peg – Springburn
Pen – Bridgeton
Penny Mob – Townhead
Port Toi – Port Dundas
Possil
Powrie – Dennistoun

Q
Queen Street Posse – city centre
Queenslie Fleet
Queenslie Rebels

R
Rebels – Rutherglen
Redskins – Southside
Romeos – Garngard
Royston Shamrock
Rutherglen Fleet

S

Sally Boys – East End
San Toi – Calton
Scurvy
Shamrock – Germiston
Shanly Boys
Sheiks – Drygate
Sheilds
Sighthill Mafia
Silver Bell
Skinheads
Skull – Bridgeton and Cathcart
Southside Stickers
Spur
Spur 78 – Barrowfield
Star – Garthamlock
Sticket – Bridgeton

T

Tay – Castlemilk
Temple
Thistle – Queen Mary Street
Thrush – Townhead
Tigers – Shettleston
Tim Malloys
Tiny Glen – Rutherglen
Tongs – Calton
Toon Tongs – Townhead/Garngad

Torch – Calton
Torran Toi – Easterhouse
Tradeston Rebels

U

Uncle – Ruchill

V

Valley – Maryhill
Village – Baillieston
Village Boys – Southside
Vordo – Govan

W

Waverley Boys
Wee Do'e Hill
Wee Men – Tollcross
Wild Team – Rutherglen
Wimpey – Dalmuir
Wine Alley – Govan

Y

Yoker Toi
Young 41
Young Fernhill Team
Young Glen – Rutherglen
Young Rolland Boys (YRB) – Ruchill
Young Team – Maryhill
YY Mods – Easterhouse

4

REDSKINS RULE

The First World War headlines, tiny by today's tabloid standards, nonetheless tell the story of "Hooliganism in Glasgow", "Racecourse Hooligans – Glasgow Men Heavily Sentenced", "Badged Rowdies – Rival Gangs in Court", "Wild scene in Glasgow", "Riotous Scenes in Rutherglen" etc, etc, etc.

Newspapers have come a long way since they first began to record the goings-on of the gangs. I once worked with a senior executive who made a point of leaving the news desk the minute his allotted shift was over. No matter the excitement of the day he rolled down his sleeves and donned his jacket. His parting words to his fellow toilers was invariably an instruction to "lead on the best story". Not the most important. The best. And to his mind the best was always a strong human interest yarn. Stories that he deemed "important but dull" got into the paper, but seldom on the front page.

Glasgow's newspapers during the First World War would have baffled him – the human interest gems were not on the front page (paying adverts took this prime spot) but even the meatiest of them were hidden behind dull tales of local politics or the pontificating of the good and the great.

However, the stories behind those well crafted but small size headlines make fascinating reading and provide insight into the crimes of the times. Around the turn of the century two particular gangs caught the attention of the papers – the San Toy Boys and the Tim Malloys. Even then slogans, war cries and chants were a feature of gang life and the San Toys were said to go about shouting, rather unimaginatively, "We are the young San Toys and we can fight the Tim Malloys".

The year 1916 for some reason saw the gangs at their worst and the early headline writers, like the journalists of today, never lightly spurned the opportunity to use clichés like "reign of terror". A gang called The Redskins featured in many court stories and were said to have their "happy hunting ground in the east end".

The reporting of the effect of the gangs was couched in pretty unspectacular language, but was deeply detailed. A *Glasgow Herald* report in June of that year with the headline "Hooliganism in Glasgow" was typical:

"A display of rowdyism, fortunately unattended by serious consequences, occurred in the Bridgeton district of Glasgow on Tuesday night. The crowd which numbered thirty or forty youths shouted and yelled as they passed along several of the leading thoroughfares to Bridgeton Cross.

"Crying 'we are the ******* Redskins', they jostled and otherwise interfered with a number of people including a gentleman who declined to give the police his name and address saying he was afraid his assailants might victimise him.

"Detective Beattie and Constable Lorimer, who were in plain clothes, followed the rowdies for some time and at Bridgeton Cross they arrested three of them on charges of breach of the peace.

"The prisoners – John Friel, 18 years of age; Archibald Fitzgerald, aged 21, and William Donnelly, aged 17, came before Bailie Kennedy at the Eastern Police court yesterday. Friel, who is said to be a recent arrival from Ireland and Fitzgerald, who said he was a music hall artiste but had been idle for about five months, were each sentenced to 14 days' imprisonment. And Donnelly, on account of his youth, was given the option of a fine of £1 1s or 14 days."

Such rowdyism was not particularly desperate, but the Redskins were into more than just bellowing gang slogans and putting the fear of death into the populace.

Extortion was also on their agenda and in the same year the *Glasgow Herald* gave a classic example. It was tucked away between adverts for a Mr F. Thompson of Gordon Street who was selling, among other things, Comfortine Foot Powder and Nervetonine, which apparently was the thing to take to keep you going if you hadn't had a holiday for years and there was not much likelihood of getting one, and other riveting information like the date of the next meeting of the Scottish Colliery Under-Managers' Association.

In the deadpan style of the era it was said that "evidence of a remarkable nature was heard in a case which came before Sheriff Lyell in Glasgow Sheriff Court when two men said to be members of the Redskins gang were convicted of assault".

The court heard that the two Redskins, in this case James Martin and John Evans, were charged with having, in concert with several others, assaulted a bookmaker at Carntyne race track.

The bookie, Arthur Green, told of a group of ten or twelve men coming up to him at the races. He saw Martin and Evans among them and knew they were members of the Redskins. The Redskins held out their hands and said "drop us a dollar". The bookie bravely but unwisely declined and the men went away. They returned later. Martin said "you are the boy who refused to give the boys a dollar". He then smashed his fist into the bookie's face, knocking him down whereupon he was given a kicking until spectators intervened. The bookie reported the incident to the police the next day.

Later he was in Main Street, Bridgeton, with another bookmaker, Frank Gilmour, when they recognised a crowd of Redskins. There were witnesses around but they ran away. Green used his stick to try to beat off the assailants who were attacking Gilmour, until the police arrived.

Gilmour told the court that at the races a man had come up and asked him for money to pay a lawyer – a request that caused laughter in court – and he had paid out to save trouble. A crowd of men then went round all the bookmakers extorting money with only Green refusing to pay.

As if this violence was not enough, the affair soon took an even nastier turn. Days later, in Bell Street, Martin and some other Redskins came upon Gilmour. Martin was said to be holding something behind his back. Gilmour rushed to a nearby close for safety and the crowd followed him and a revolver was fired. Gilmour ran up the stairs and barricaded himself behind a door until the police arrived.

But safety was hard to find in Bridgeton these days. And Gilmour and Green were again attacked in the street later that night.

The sheriff sentenced each accused to six months. This sort of thing could not be tolerated on the streets of Glasgow he said. True, but he then added a postscript that is hard to swallow: "Until this case I had no idea that there were people who called themselves this and gangs who went about interfering with other people in the transaction of their business." A sheltered life or what?

Imagine what today's papers would have made of such incidents – revolvers brandished, a victim of the mob running for safety and a siege up tenement stairs. But it was all presented as pretty weak ale during the First World War when presumably minds were concentrated elsewhere and when deaths in the mud of Europe's trenches were counted in the millions.

A coup of sorts for the Redskins was taking "possession" of a tram. This incident happened in Dalmarnock Road in the vicinity of Farme Cross. The Redskins had been "in conflict with some other combination" when they stormed the tramcar with the passengers scarpering for their lives. A huge crowd had gathered to watch the rumble which seemed to have its origins in a dispute on which group had booked the nearby Steel's Hall for a Sunday night dance. The police were called, the tram was liberated and two of the Redskins arrested. They had on their persons weapons which were considered dangerous, but no details were given.

When these two thugs appeared in court, a couple of their gang pals were also in the dock, accused of assaulting a father and son at a football match in Southcroft Park. One of them was said to be a ringleader of the Redskins and to have committed the assault with a steel baton and the other was said to have fired a revolver.

Reports of assaults like this kill any notion that the gangs only fought among themselves. At times during the First World War you took your life in your hands if you went to the greyhound racing, a football match or even a tram trip into town. Ordinary folk were often at real risk when the gangs started to battle. The scale of some of these battles has to a certain extent been forgotten. The Redskins are said to have had around 1,000 members during the First World War and were well organised with a strict hierarchy. The *Bulletin* newspaper, now no longer published, called them a "nefarious organisation" and they had a peculiar whistle used by gang members to call others to their aid in times of difficulty. The history of the Redskins seems at variance with the widely held belief that the pre-Second World War gangs were composed mostly of unemployed and desperate men. But the number of female gang members was also a major concern to the authorities and the *People's Journal* talked of pretty girl hooligans and claimed that in some gangs there were more females than males and the gang structure included "queens as well as kings". The press reports show that the gangs were responsible for extortion on shopkeepers – not just bookmakers – and assaults on the police as well as members of the public. One court case tells of a Redskin leader attacking a man with a knife in one hand and bottle in the other.

Burglary, too, was on the menu. In one sheriff court sitting two groups of young people, twenty in all, and said to be members of Bridgeton's Kill Me Deads and the Baltic Fleet, appeared charged with housebreaking in the east end. One of the groups – described as five boys and two girls – admitted charges of stealing brandy, whisky, port and wines from a Rutherglen shop during night raids. One of the youths, aged 16, was described as an incorrigible rascal and sent to prison with hard labour for six months. The ages of those charged ranged from just fourteen to thirty-two. In one case the plate glass window of a spirit shop was smashed and the gang just piled in and helped themselves. The sheriff advised the accused to give up association with "such stupid people as those who by calling themselves by ridiculous names thought to make themselves heroes and heroines. They were only poor vulgar thieves who took what did not belong to them from out of the pockets of people who worked." Most of the boys were jailed but the girls who ran with them were dealt with by "severe admonishment".

Talking of ridiculous names, many Glasgow citizens had never heard of the Bloodhound Flying Corps until their members started to make regular court appearances charged with violent offences. Just how dangerous the weapons used by these thugs could be was brought out in one case. Albert Gallagher, Patrick McGrory and John Dunn, three young men, all members of the Bloodhound Flying Corps, were charged with breach of the peace in Greendyke Street. Weapons mentioned at their trial included "a hammer, a piece of stick loaded with lead, a heavy bolt attached to a waxed thread, and an iron bolt attached to string". Incidentally, in time honoured fashion, the mothers of two of the accused appeared in court to say that their boys were hard working lads who supported the family. The thugs said the weapons were for protection. The verdict: Guilty.

The pre-Second World War courts were full of young men on charges resulting from gang fights. The numbers involved are on occasion staggering. In one case in the thirties four young men belonging to the Cheeky Forty were found guilty of mobbing and rioting and were given six months with hard labour. According to the court report, "women friends of the accused became hysterical on the announcement of the sentence and had to be assisted out in a grief stricken state. One woman collapsed in her seat and had to be carried unconscious in a faint to an ante-room where she received attention." A police constable from the Northern Division gave a dramatic account of the gang fight which took place at 10.30 p.m. on a Saturday night. A riotous mob had gathered in Castle Street, Monkland Street and Parliamentary Road. About 300 people were involved in the fight. The PC said: "The crowd which was composed fairly equally of men and women was swaying from one side of the street to another. Bottles and stones and other missiles were being thrown freely in the fight." The constable said the four accused were prominent members of the Cheeky Forty and there was no doubt about their identity. But another constable explained his inability to get witnesses from the crowd to give evidence by stating that local people were terrified by the gangs. "You get shopkeepers complaining about the Cheeky Forty gang coming to their shops to ask for money to pay their fines."

The Cheeky Forty were seldom out of trouble and they seemed to have some foresight in their battles. In yet another Saturday night rumble they took on members of the Row Amateur Social Club in Cathedral Street. This time the weapons found after the dust had cleared were beer bottles, pieces of wood, parts of billiard cues, an iron bar, a baton, a bamboo stick, part of a barber's pole, and a piece of metal shaped like a dagger. When the culprits reached court it was said that when the police arrived and realised the size of the battle they could not immediately summon help as the combatants had taken the precaution of cutting the wires in the nearby phone kiosk.

All this was long before Lord Carmont and his policy of heavy sentences but one Sheriff Fyffe seemed to be a lawman of similar stripe. According to the *Herald* he was in favour of drastic measures – "methods more Cromwellian than courts of law can exercise" – to curb the hooligan gangs of the time.

This early hammer of the neds made his comments as eight young men came before him in the County Buildings charged with breach of the peace and disorderly conduct on the north bank of the Clyde and elsewhere in the Bridgeton district on a Sunday afternoon in September 1916.

One of the accused was in a soldier's uniform and the others – including the accusers – wore "munitions workers' badges". Three youths stated that on the afternoon in question they were set upon by individual members of a crowd of around fifty lads. They were beaten on the head with bottles, bolts and other weapons. They denied that they were members of the Bell-on gang and one of

54

them said he knew that one of the attacking crowd was a member of the Redskins.

A female mill worker who was with the assaulted youths said that when she saw the crowd coming towards them she remarked: "Here's the Baltic Fleet". This caused some laughter in court. She then recognised one of the accused and said, "No, it's the Skins". More laughter in court.

The sheriff said at the close that he thought it high time the police authorities made a report to the Minister of Munitions in regard to certain young men who were working in munitions work and, he supposed, making big money, and in their time off on Sundays disgracing the city with their disorderly conduct. The Minister of Munitions had the power to badge men and the power to debadge men. He also had the power to bring men back home from the army for munitions work.

The exercise of such powers would have been a shorter and more effective way of putting down the rowdyism which seemed to exist in the east end of Glasgow than jailing sections of one gang or the other. And asking the court to decide from most unsatisfactory and most contradictory evidence whether half a dozen or so were identified as part of a crowd of sixty committing a breach of the peace or whether some of them assaulted some of the sixty crowd. The sheriff in this particular case then thundered: "It is high time these disturbers of the peace were debadged and sent to do their bit at the front and that decent men who have already done their bit in France were released from the colours to take the place of the hooligans."

He then made the not entirely original observation that the sort of street fighting man brought before the courts in Glasgow would most probably make a really good soldier. A point that would find agreement with those unfortunate to tangle with the "poison dwarfs" who found their way into many a Scottish regiment and struck fear into the unfortunates who had to do battle with them! The memory of the fearsome reputation of the brave and big-hearted, if short in stature, squaddies of the Highland Light Infantry who trained in Maryhill barracks, lives on as strongly in some parts of Germany as it does in Glasgow.

5

BILLY BOYS
AND NORMAN CONKS

Main Street, Bridgeton is still, in 2002, a depressing sight. Efforts
to build some new housing and to raise the standards in the area
have had only marginal effect. It is now something of a tatty litter-
strewn thoroughfare to be driven through as speedily as possible
en route to Rutherglen or the impressive detached homes of
Cambuslang, Burnside, or even the new town of East Kilbride to
which many a Brigton denizen was decanted.

Much is made by sociologists and criminologists of the
deprivation of areas like Bridgeton and the part it played in
spawning crime, but there are not too many first hand accounts of
what life was really like. One exception is a thirties newspaper
report of the return to Bridgeton of an exile who had left many
years before, but could remember what it was like in the dying
years of the nineteenth century. He describes the sanitary
arrangements as a disgrace to a civilised country. He remembers
young girls with bare heads, shoulder shawls or plaids. They wore
cotton "shorguns" (short gowns), stiff thibet petticoats bulging out
all round the bottom. They were often barefooted. They started
work in cotton mills and weaving factories at 6 a.m. (rise at 5) and
worked till 6 p.m. for a pittance of 7–8 shillings a week. Children
of ten or eleven, known as half-timers, worked for 2s or 3s a week.
Young men wore bell-bottomed trousers flapping around the
ankles, a knitted "grauvit" (muffler) and what were described as
"hooker doon" or "kill me dead" caps. The exile remembered

prize-fights on a site near Springfield Road on Sundays –
arrangements were made for the next Sunday to sort out fights
among the spectators. These were described as real he-man affairs
with contestants stripped to the waist and smiting each other with
lunging bare-knuckle blows cheered on by supporters and
gamblers. Another memory of the east end was of the "rat pit" at
Bernard Street. Here you could buy a live rat to use to train your
terrier as a rat catcher. Or you could gamble on how many rats a
dog could kill in a given time. According to this observer, who
perhaps fancied himself as an archaeologist, the housing conditions
were worse than Skara Brae. This was not much of an exaggeration:
in 1911 it was reported that in Broomielaw ward seventy-three out
of every hundred houses made human life "indecent and painful".
And in the twenties 60,000 Glaswegians marched against landlords'
attempts to increase rents. A Govan tenant pursued for rent arrears
of 9d – around 4p – told a court he refused to pay on principle. "I
was having my breakfast when a rat came in and ate my ham." In
the late twenties a government report showed that 13 per cent of
Glaswegians lived in single-ends – the highest proportion in the
UK. Even in 1976 Glasgow had almost half a million substandard
houses and there were almost 50,000 families on the waiting list.
And nostalgia for the comradeships of the old days of bad housing
can be much overdone. One eminent toiler in the field of public
health called the tenements "castles of misery" and was much
motivated in his work by the plight of toddlers trapped in them,
unable to see "moon or stars".

Illegal gambling was a major problem in the poorer areas of
Glasgow and not just on the result of prize-fights. As a boy my
father and I split our football affiliations between Third Lanark,
now defunct, and Clyde FC, now in the new town of Cumbernauld.
Neat scheduling by the often criticised football authorities allowed
us to visit Cathkin Park one Saturday and Shawfield at the bottom
of Main Street in Bridgeton the next, one of the advantages of
growing up as a southsider. However occasional visits to the big
boys at Ibrox or Parkhead were often in order and I well remember

my father pointing out waste ground near Springfield Road where, he told me, there had been a flapping track where the working man raced whippets for big bets. Similar areas were used for pitch and toss sessions again with what Damon Runyon liked to call "coarse notes" changing hands. Such alfresco gambling was not just an east end thing. There was what the press called a "rendezvous for sporting men" on the banks of the Forth and Clyde Canal on open ground near Ellesmere Street, Maryhill. It was subject to regular police raids and as many as twenty men at a time were arrested for "having formed part of a disorderly crowd who conducted themselves in a disorderly manner, engaging in various forms of gaming and committed a breach of the peace". A police witness pointed out that this space was frequented by men who were able to catch a fleeting glimpse of the dog racing in Firhill Park and "the shouting was loudest when the races were in progress". No surprise there!

My own early memories of Main Street, Bridgeton, are less dramatic. Here lived my aunt Meg who had come with the rest of her family from rural Ulster. Her brothers were staunch Protestants said to have signed the pledge in their own blood. The place was no paradise, but it was lively and vibrant in a way it isn't today. There was a bustle and energy that has gone, replaced with boarded windows and an air of hopelessness. But even in the forties and fifties it was no easy place to scratch a living and most of Meg's many brothers had long departed to the North Sea trawlers working out of Hull or to the liners that still, in these days, plied between Britain and its Empire or to some dull factory in the Midlands. It kept them out of trouble and out of the gangs. But memories of life in Ulster and its bigotry were deeply ingrained in the area. Meg, a lovely aunt and a fine person in most respects, but a victim of her heritage, looked forward with longing to one day each summer – the twelfth of July.

"Window hinging" was a great Glasgow institution and Meg loved nothing better than to lean out, arms folded on the ledge of her tenement window, in classic pose, and watch the Orange parades march noisily down Main Street. She talked about nothing else for weeks before and afterwards, especially of the performance of such characters as the legendary Orange minister Alan Hasson – later to fall from grace – heading the parade riding a magnificent white horse with the flute bands blasting their music back off the walls of the narrow tenement streets. A detour or two down streets known to be the haunts of Catholics was a must. But this was not without risk and the violence was far from one-sided. A classic example of this is recalled in Percy Sillitoe's book telling the inside story of his battle against the city's warring factions. The legendary gang-buster wrote about events in 1935. On Catholic Holy days the Billy Boys gang organised a drum and flute band and marched through Norman Street playing inflammatory party tunes. "As soon as the offensive music was heard by the Norman Conks, they manned the upper windows and even the roofs in their streets and when the Billy Boys band tried to march past, it was met by downpour of bricks, missiles, buckets of filth and broken glass. If the Norman Conks could have made boiling lead I am sure they would not have hesitated to use that, too. It was certainly all that would have been needed to complete the picture of a medieval siege."

The police moved in on this particular battle and Sir Percy felt that this incident was the beginning of the end for the Billy Boys as the pre-eminent gang. A mounted police charge (Sillitoe's Cossacks as they were nicknamed) broke up the parade, resulting in total victory for the boys in blue. No quarter seems to have been asked or given and Sillitoe wrote that: "Only one of the Billy Boys escaped injury. He was Elijah Cooper the big drum player. When the police charged Elijah dived into his drum and used it as shelter until he could surrender peacefully."

Such was the heritage of hatred and bigotry in Bridgeton that Orange parades continued in the fifties, if in less violent form. This was years after the Second World War when Bridgeton folk had fought side by side against a common enemy and after years of assimilation and much effort in education. What it must have really been like in the twenties and thirties is hard to fully comprehend.

Later in life William Fullerton, the founder and leader of the Billy Boys, looked back through somewhat rose-tinted spectacles at the gang's heyday in a series of articles in the old *Evening Citizen*, from the Beaverbrook stable, when the city could boast three evening papers. *Times, News* and *Citi-zennn* was the cry from the street corner vendors. Davie Stewart, a highly experienced reporter, had the confidence of the old gangster and recorded much of the history of the gang.

But Fullerton hadn't been paying much attention to what was going on in the streets and courts of Glasgow and his stamping ground of Bridgeton in particular in the years leading up to the violent twenties and thirties. The gangster told Stewart that Bridgeton in the twenties was as orderly as any Glasgow district. "True it was possible to lose your gold watch if you had one, and one Glasgow bailie of the day did, and have it returned the next day if you knew the right people to approach. But crime and violence did not rear an aggressive head!"

The gangster gospel according to King Billy himself was that all was sweetness and light until a certain football match in which he starred was held in the Green. The year was 1924 and one team was called Kent Star and the other just a bunch of eleven Bridgeton lads who didn't mind much what they were called.

Fullerton – full of vitality and with it that little bit of extra fire which was to have its pains and penalties later, said the reporter – was a mere eighteen years old.

And the youngster committed the first of many mistakes. He actually scored a goal against the rival gang team. And Kent Star had followers and supporters that you upset at your own risk. Fullerton was marked out for special attention – an attack by hammer wielding Kent Star men.

Fullerton survived and vowed revenge. With a group of around thirty like-minded youngsters a new gang was born: the Brigton Billy Boys. With the ferocity of pack animals the Billy Boys set about putting Glasgow to rights and Fullerton, deemed the most powerful fighter, became leader. The growth of the gang was truly awesome. Within a short time they had around 800 members. Such was their infamy that they recruited from Airdrie, Coatbridge and Cambuslang as well as the tenements of Main Street and its surroundings. There were battles around the Green and on Rutherglen Bridge involving hundreds of men.

They built up an arsenal of hammers, hatchets, bayonets from the First World War, and even Indian clubs, intended as a keep-fit aid, were pressed into service. Bottles, lead-filled sticks and huge bolts were also handy weapons. And the cut-throat razor was beginning to become a weapon of choice. One occasion was a memorable indication of this. Fullerton was playing for a football team called Kimberly against the old rivals Kent Star. When the Kimberly centre-half clashed with the opposing centre-forward a razor fell from the pocket of his football strip. In his *Citizen* articles William Fullerton went along with the thinking that unemployment had much to do with the violence. Gang battles were a regular occurrence, especially with the rival Norman Conks. Fullerton believed all this activity was an antidote to the boredom of unemployment. Excitement was on tap.

The Billy Boys filled the non-fighting part of their life with a training regime that was perhaps one of their attractions to fit young men at a loose end. They met regularly in a hall in London Road and Billy was in charge of the parade ground. He told Davie Stewart: "I drilled them like a battalion of soldiers. Many of them had already experienced discipline in Borstal and I took advantage of the fact." Fullerton was also secretary and treasurer of the "organisation". They had secret bank accounts accessible only to Fullerton and two loyal lieutenants in which considerable sums of money were kept. This was unique among the gangs who tended to rob and extort and simply trouser the proceeds. The Billy Boys had membership cards and members paid a small sum weekly. In an echo of the Penny Mob this went to pay fines and help families when a slip of a hammer or hatchet on to the skull of a rival sent some "loved one" away for a spell in the Bar-L. Some of the cash, of course, came from illegal activities. And some of it was spent on an unlikely purchase – musical instruments. Fullerton thought the fighting was developing a boring sameness and came up with the idea of a flute band to keep the lads interested!

Many of the gang could play musical instruments and here was a chance to really annoy the Catholics of Bridgeton. This was a time of change; the bigotry came into the foreground. A visit to Belfast was arranged to learn from the world's leading exponents how such musical taunting should be done. The visit may have been a success musically but two gang members were injured in a shooting incident.

The musical side to the Billy Boys was of some importance in the structure of the gang. Even Percy Sillitoe thought they were "genuine musicians in a rough way". And after meetings of the gang were over they stood in all weathers at Bridgeton Cross and played "God Save the King".

With the rose-coloured spectacles on, Fullerton still insisted that the streets were safe enough if you were discreet enough not to display "party colours", which presumably meant even a hint of green and white could provoke mayhem. But there was no denying that even the dole paid to the unemployed was a source of violence. Gangs hung around the "buroo" waiting for the opposition to turn up to claim their money. Pitched battles resulted with claimants for the government's cash having to fight their way in and out of the "buroo".

The public followed all this from the safety of an armchair and the newspapers which charted battles, fines and sentences in great detail.

But usually all was well if you kept your head down, although the gangsters themselves rarely went out without some form of weaponry. Attacks in the street were commonplace and miscreants recognised each other and old scores were settled violently, there and then. William Fullerton told Davie Stewart of the *Citizen* one remarkable tale of a wedding in 1926 of one of the Boys. The bridegroom stood before the minister with a sword concealed in his morning dress. The best man had a gun in his pocket. Outside the church the Calton Entry waited for the nuptials to be completed. When the wedding party came out the Calton boys threw bottles, not confetti. It makes the Wild West sound tame, and Fullerton topped his wedding finery with a blood soaked bandage. He had had fifteen stitches put in a head wound a few days earlier. After the ceremony there was a running battle till the Billy Boys reached the sanctuary of a Masonic hall in Struthers Street where the reception went ahead as normal. You wonder what the speeches were like. Incidentally although the Calton Entry were primarily a Catholic gang, like many of their rivals the religious element was sometimes tenuous. Indeed the Entry at one time boasted a Protestant as one of their best fighters.

Fullerton was also responsible for a sinister little offshoot of the Billy Boys – the Ku Klux Klan. It met in the Foundry Boys Hall in London Road and was said to have similar aims to the Billy Boys, presumably violence and bigotry mixed with some pseudo soldiering and musical interludes. The members took an oath of allegiance and paid 2d a week. They wore black and white ties and "K" badges made especially for them by a local tradesman. But the Klan didn't seem to create the same loyalty as their seniors and most of the members in time joined the senior arm, and the Klan withered as a separate entity.

But if the Glasgow Klan under Fullerton was nothing to be compared with the real Klan who terrorised the blacks in the deep south in America with their wizards, robes and burning crosses, the Billy Boys still had some pretty sinister friends.

King Billy Fullerton joined the British Fascist Party and became a section commander with 200 men and women under his command. But by 1955 he was telling the papers that: "I couldn't give you the definition of a fascist to this day. It just seemed like a good thing to belong to at the time." Seems Sir Oswald Mosley's anti-Semitism and support for Hitler, if not the Englishman's taste for street violence, had passed him by.

The other political enemy was of course the Communist Party and Fullerton's black shirted troops had one notable battle with a Communist Party procession. Right from the start the fascists had their eye on the rival party's big drum. It soon became part of the Billy Boys band.

Interestingly, "respectable" politicians were not above using the Billy Boys to disrupt rivals' meetings.

The Billy Boys would fight anyone who would fight them, but their legendary opponents were the Norman Conks, whose weapons of choice were pickshafts weighing nearly three pounds and measuring 42 inches in length. Hatchets, sharpened bicycle chains and swords were also used by the Conks and the Billy Boys. Beer bottles had their uses, too. Unlike a gun or a knife you were unlikely to be in trouble with the law for simply carrying one. Unopened it was a useful club. Smashed open its jagged edges could scalp or disfigure an opponent and, of course, it was a cheap missile. No less than Sir Percy Sillitoe has attested to the Conks' ruthlessness in fighting back and their leader, Bull Bowman, was a formidable and frightening figure despite attracting less attention from the general public and the press than Fullerton. Fullerton, though, was not a criminal in the accepted sense but a fighting man who enjoyed pitting his men against the Conks. He steered clear of thieving and had only a minor conviction for assault. Sillitoe thought his generalship was both ingenious and reckless.

Fullerton's rule of the Billy Boys really ended with an arrest in remarkable circumstances. On his own patch, drunk and surrounded by his men, he was carrying a baby (why is unclear!). A brave policeman asked him to put it down and when he refused, the PC accused him of being drunk in charge of a baby. A riot ensued but the police, though outnumbered and faced with an assortment of gang weapons, won through. When the case came to court a number of witnesses told of being hit by Big Tommy of the Toll and that was the last they remembered. Eventually the magistrate asked, who is this Big Tommy? The arresting police officer, Police Sergeant Morrison stood up. Sillitoe records that the magistrate took one look at the huge "polisman" and said "I think I begin to understand".

The baby who started this particular rammy is nameless but King Billy spawned a lawless dynasty. His son died in a stabbing in James Street, Bridgeton in 1994 and his grandson also made headlines in a shooting in the Candleriggs.

The old gang leader, much mellowed, died in 1962 aged 57. He got a send off he would have appreciated. A strong police presence was there to control the crowds – around 1,000 gathered to see the funeral party leave a Bridgeton tenement en route to Riddrie cemetery. The traffic was stopped at Bridgeton Cross – scene of many affrays between the Boys and the Conks – by the procession. The Billy Boys may have passed into history, but their musical memory lives on in hate-filled football chants. And music played a role till the end. For part of the way the funeral procession was headed by a flute band. The records don't say where the big drum came from. Or who the drummer was. But its sombre beat closed an infamous episode in Glasgow's history.

Fullerton and Bowman are perhaps the best remembered of the old time gang leaders. But others had great notoriety in their day, like Peter Williamson the leader of the Beehive gang. This gang, like many others, started as a group of men with time on their hands hanging around street corners. Indeed the gang was originally called the Beehive Corner Boys. According to Sillitoe the inner circle of this group were housebreakers but around them moved a group of men ready for fights, intimidation, mob attacks and robberies. An interesting character, Williamson was said to be well educated, intelligent and a fluent speaker who came from a respectable family. He was so mentally agile that he could put up a good show defending himself in court, something he often got the chance to do.

He obviously had some style, for Sillitoe in his book telling of his time gang busting in Glasgow, records that he was expert in spotting the arrival of the police at the scene of an affray. When the boys in blue started to wade into the miscreants Williamson was often found eloquently appealing to the brawling gangs to behave themselves. The peacemaker pose, usually adopted with the pavement around him littered with bruised bodies of rival gangsters he had coshed, often saved him from arrest.

But it was a role with a limited run. After a while he became a well known face to the police. And the old lies wouldn't work. Other Beehive members who crop up in the story of the era include Harry M'Menemy who was Williamson's lieutenant. So loyal was Harry that it is said he once pleaded guilty to a crime committed by Williamson since he had fewer convictions and would get off more lightly.

The fighting culture of these days is remarkable. In his autobiography Sillitoe tells of one youngster who ran with the gangs and was not considered anything special as a fighter yet won the welterweight Scottish boxing championship.

Another gang leader of the time was James Dalziel of the Parlour Boys whose H.Q. was the Bedford Parlour Dance Hall in Celtic Street. Amazing as it seems now, this fellow, known as Razzle Dazzle, considered it too effeminate to dance with girls and chose his partners from burly gangsters. He died in a bloody brawl with San Toy members in the dance hall, stabbed in the throat.

The details of this particular murder give insight into what such a gang fight was really like. Dalziel lived in Surrey Street with his wife and four children. After his killing no fewer than sixteen men appeared in court and the fatal blow was said to have come from a stab wound or razor slash. The dance that night had been in progress for some time when a number of youths forced their way in and started trouble. The whole place swiftly erupted into a general melee and witnesses said the weapons used included bottles, razors and knives. The newspapers reported that screaming women huddled together to avoid the fighting men and several young girls fainted and required attention. Dalziel received severe throat injuries and died in the Victoria Infirmary shortly after being taken there on the back of a passing lorry.

A huge police operation was mounted with the entire staff of the city's CID department involved at all hours over the weekend. An identity parade – perhaps the largest ever held in the city – took place. Almost 100 of the young men and women who had been at the dance took part. For more than two hours the dancers who had had their night out so bloodily interrupted were at the Southern police station while detectives pursued their inquiry. When the accused finally appeared in court they were all said to be in their twenties and two appeared with bloodstained bandaged heads.

In the almost traditional, to this day, Glasgow gesture of the hard man in court, they were said to have waved cheerily to their friends who were there. The prosecution faced enormous difficulties in such gang fights whether in dance halls or in Glasgow Green or the streets. It was almost impossible to find out who actually did what in such a battle when a large group of combatants struck out with razors, bottles, and knives, not to mention chains, axes and hammers.

It was no great surprise that in an unedifying final twist to this particular tale, the man said to have struck the killer blow at Razzle Dazzle managed to get the jury on his side and dodge the rope, escaping the final sanction for murder.

6

BATTLES ON THE HOME FRONT

Two repeating threads wind their way through any history of Glasgow's gangland: the nature of the causes of such massive violence, and a concern as to what to do about it, other than keep on jailing the perpetrators.

Down the years sheriffs and high court judges alike have pontificated that "such behaviour will not be tolerated in this city", "violence must be stamped out", etc. That has been the cry from the bench for more than a hundred years.

But still the gangs run. Albeit in a different form, they are still around in Glasgow as in most other large cities with similar problems. Time after time it has been claimed that the gangs have been smothered to death. But somehow they draw oxygen from somewhere and rise again.

It has not been for want of trying by the legal system, the police or the general public. Concern about the problem has been a priority down the years for reformers as well as the hard tickets on the right side of the law who wanted to meet violence with violence.

During the First World War there was evidence of clear thinking on hooliganism in many letters in the press debating the problem. Many were constructive and sympathetic with regard to the youngsters who joined gangs in search of "amusement and adventure". The latter day reflections of Billy Fullerton of the Billy Boys confirm that lack of direction in their lives made the gang structure an appealing prospect to spirited young men, and occasionally girls.

In July 1916 the *Herald* published an important and lengthy letter from a Mr H. Campbell writing from an address at 156 St Vincent Street. The good Mr Campbell wrote to the editor:

"A great deal has been written of late in your columns on the increase in our city of hooliganism.

"While in no way seeking to make light of these outbreaks or offences I would like to put in a plea for the working lad of our poorer classes who is too often looked upon and described as a hooligan by those who have little sympathy, less acquaintance and no knowledge of his upbringings, surroundings or needs.

"Juvenile crime has little to do with special depravity, but very much to do with parental neglect and bad example, upbringing in a one or two roomed house where the kitchen forms the nursery, dining room, scullery, sitting room, bathroom and bedroom all in one.

"Where in the name of reason is there space for a boy to grow up, with all the expected virtues so often found wanting even in the lad from a better class home. If troublesome it is 'away out and play', if hungry a piece of bread is given to be eaten outside, if fractious a 'clout on the ear' and a shove out the door."

The author of this intriguing epistle goes on to talk of the problems of a youngster set free from the discipline of school at fourteen and turned adrift to earn a few coppers from whatever work he can find as a newsvendor, van boy or delivery lad. "Is it any wonder that at the all too critical time in a boy's life, having such home surroundings and bursting with animal spirits, he occasionally breaks out in a display of hooliganism? The wonder to me is that the tens of thousands of city working lads are so well behaved."

Few could argue with this cogent analysis of the problem but Mr Campbell has solutions on offer as well: properly equipped lads' clubs in the "densest parts of our working class districts where the lads could have an outlet for their vitality. Better opportunities for games, gymnastics, and drill. Where discipline would be learned and lads taught the benefits of a clean body, strong muscles and a developed chest."

This elegant exposition of the fact that the devil makes work for idle hands touched a cord with his fellow citizens and such thinking had, of course, much to do with the rise of Scouting and the Boy's Brigade.

One writer, from the wealthy avenues of Kelvinside, had a further idea. Get the youngsters out into fresh air on Saturdays and Sundays. According to this correspondent the lack of a decent train service on a Sunday made it difficult for lads to access the "beautiful and healthy countryside that surrounds Glasgow". His solution: "permanent weekend camps in the wastelands of the hills with small fixed charges for food and accommodation. And factories employing lads should provide a games field for their boys."

Another letter writer perceptively picked up a point about the Scouts, BB, the various Guilds and YMCA and their inability to attract the people who need them most. John Chambers of Greenlaw Manse, Paisley said that "Properly equipped lads' clubs run by even the most enthusiastic, will do no more than touch the fringe of evil because such clubs do not get the lads who most need the discipline."

Presumably Mr Chambers was not in his pulpit when he wrote that what was needed was "a moral revolution making our street corners safe and preparing a generation of men who will uphold the traditions of our country in workshop and in yard as in ironclad and trench". But he could have been.

However this was not mere rhetoric. He believed that if school boards would only make night school compulsory for fourteen- to eighteen-year olds hooliganism would wane.

In the great traditions of newspapers as a debating society this brought a blast back from Mr Campbell who was well known for his work among the poorer youths in the city slums. In reply to the Paisley minister's suggestion he wrote that "the school boards have been wise in not attempting to make full use of their compulsory powers. To keep the lad working from 6 a.m. to 5 p.m.

then compel him to spend the evening in a schoolroom without providing facilities for social recreation would be out of the question. All work and no play won't do." Something of a visionary, Mr Campbell found the *Herald* on his side in this debate with a thundering piece of leader writing.

August 2, 1916, was what they call in the trade a busy news day. The Russians were pressing forward on the Stockhod front according to unconfirmed reports and in the Commons Mr Chamberlain read a telegram from the Government of India on a troop train disaster. At Buckingham Palace the King and Queen inspected a gift of fifty ambulances from India. Nonetheless the *Herald* devoted much of the most important page in the paper to a leader on "The Ethics of Physical Discipline".

Mrs Thatcher, famous for her contention that there is no such thing as society, would have been unamused. "The hooligan, the common rough of the common street, is not entirely a police problem. The sins of the rough are interrelated with the sins of society: his existence in the communal state is a reproach as well as a menace to our social order" declaimed the *Herald*.

Firmly on the side of Mr Campbell, it concluded: "The training that makes for physical dignity can not fail to have a reflex action on conduct. The element of physical training, greatly developed, ought to be made an integral and vital part of our system of elementary education." Wise words. But sadly it would take more than physical training to wipe out hooliganism and prevent like-minded, if misguided, youths directing their animal vitality into gangs and street fighting. Incidentally during this period the Scouting movement under Baden-Powell devised a scheme that had some success under which each scout was required to bring along a member of the "hooligan class" to meetings. Not particularly politically correct, but to a degree effective.

This need to provide youth with a more productive environment wasn't just recognised at local level. The Government of the day was drawn in. The Home Secretary, Herbert Samuel, got his officials to write to the papers, asking them to publish an invitation to the

Boys' and Girls' Brigades and clubs to go down to London for a conference. The leaders of the youth organisations were told that the Home Secretary himself would be present and that he hoped they could attend and give the Government the "benefit of their advice". An early example of listening government!

The letter eloquently detailed the Minister's concern about the growth of juvenile crime. Acknowledging that much of the trouble was the lack of social workers because of the war, the letter praised the work of the youth organisations of the time and suggested "that a conference of leaders of various great bodies concerned with social and religious work among young boys might result in a scheme for special co-operation and organisation which might materially help solve a difficult problem". Pointing out the shortage of volunteers because of the number of men at the front, the Home Secretary tried to recruit people unfit for fighting in the trenches for this battle against juvenile crime by saying that "there is no finer alternative to service at the front than helping to mould the character of the boys who are in danger of being left entirely to their own resources".

That the problem was serious there was no doubt. The Government's figures showed that, in a survey of eighteen towns, in the period December 1915 to February 1919 the youth crime rate rose from 2,686 to 3,598. The feeling was that much of this was because youngsters were being left to their own devices. But another cause for concern was raised – the influence of crime films in the cinema. All this emerged at the London conference chaired by Herbert Samuel. In the unlikely event that the delegates were not aware of what was going on, the Home Secretary produced a remarkable set of figures showing the effect of darkened streets, lack of police and social workers, mothers at munitions and other war works and fathers in the army. Boys and girls under the age of fourteen were getting involved in serious crime and youth leaders were urged to come up with ideas to stem the flow. The Home Secretary had one solid suggestion of his own – he was to introduce a central office of cinema censorship. In his view the existing local schemes weren't effective. Chief constables up and down the land had been lobbied for their views and to a man they thought the cinema was contributing to a sense of lawlessness among the young. The censorship was to apply to both films and posters.

This great debate on how to prevent idle hands doing evil was conducted in the press with the background of hundreds of thousands dying in a world war. And the work of the youth organisations clearly helped with the problems at home. Every youngster steered away from gangs and criminality was a victory. But the fact remains that all this energy and breast beating on behalf of "hooligan boys and girls" was followed just a few years later by the most serious outbreak of gang violence in the city's history. It is a sobering thought that when the gangs were at their peak, in the twenties and thirties, many of the members had been at their most impressionable during the First World War.

The urge, when faced with a problem, to call a conference was as strong in the past as it is today. Towards the end of the war a meeting of representatives of various organisations engaged in social and religious work among boys and girls in the city was convened in the City Chambers. The Town Clerk, Sir John Lindsay, presided and it was decided to form a Juvenile Organisation Committee. The meeting was also concerned with the working of the probation system. Indeed Glasgow had been a pioneer in the use of probation as a weapon against juvenile crime. One of the main speakers was Robert Holmes of Sheffield, a city that seemed to have had similar problems to Glasgow and a city that also utilised the services of Percy Sillitoe in the role of gangbuster. A man of long experience, Holmes told the conference that what was required "was a return to the attitude of heart and mind that our forefathers called fear of God". In his view the good influence of teachers was to a large extent nullified by the evil influence of the street and the home in slum areas. He asserted that this must not be allowed to continue and what the Boy's Brigade and kindred organisations were doing for a certain number of lads must also be done for those for whom "at present no one cared".

If an offence was not too grave he favoured probation, but more serious crimes meant reform school, and he believed in the "birch rod" in cases where the authorities thought it would be effective.

A strong thread of compassionate social concern weaves its way through these early reports of efforts to help the poor and deprived youth. A cleric, the Rev. Dr Wells told the conference of many cases where boys had "risen to prominence from very unpromising surroundings and averred that to help the young you had to engage them and get alongside them. This was, he said, work that brought brightness into many lives. Dr Neilson, a stipendiary magistrate, was in favour of sending potential offenders to private homes "where in most cases they would have every chance of becoming creditable members of society".

Apart from the probation service Glasgow was a visionary pace setter in what would now be seen as career guidance. Around this time there was also in existence sixteen "After Care Committees" attached to labour exchanges. The idea was to steer youngsters into jobs that reflected their abilities and had long term prospects rather than short term financial gain. The overriding notion being that this could have an effect on juvenile crime.

Around the time pupils were due to leave school, they and their parents were invited to the labour exchange to discuss their prospects. A large army of volunteer "visitors" had been recruited to help. Once the youngster started work they were under the supervision of the volunteers who went to their homes to "ascertain how the boy or girl is progressing at work and try to interest them in evening classes and guide them in making the most profitable use of their leisure". When it started there was concern that the parents would think these home visits intrusive, but in most cases it was a friendly affair. And the committee found that even if the parents were indifferent the youngsters themselves were happy with the guidance and the chance to avoid dead end jobs. It is no surprise that in Glasgow the preferred occupation for a boy was engineering.

Worthy, and successful in individual cases, as these efforts were, the problem of youth unemployment was virtually impossible to eradicate. Not long after these efforts Glasgow newspapers were still able to report that "in districts like the Gorbals, the Calton, or Bridgeton, one can see at any time of the day, but especially in the afternoon from midday till 3.30, and again in the evening, countless groups of young men and boys standing at every corner and in between.

"The casual observer mistakes these groups for the gangs. They are merely the unemployed – quiet, submissive, depressed. The only bright gleam in their eye is to be seen from twelve to three. It is the gleam of hope. Their horse may win."

This particular observer pointed out that at the time of writing, August 1930, the gangs were only seen when on the warpath as he put it. "It is only by close and careful investigation and a very cautious approach that one can get into contact with them.

"To every stranger they are on their guard. One has to cultivate their acquaintance very carefully and use many wiles before the slightest confidence is shown. Even the youths of a district who are not in the gang themselves, but know the members personally, will not give away their names and addresses."

This anonymous investigator obviously used suitable wiles and persevered to the point where he met some gang members. In a curious turn of phrase he remarked on their ordinariness and youngsters who gave the impression of "being lambs without a shepherd".

He observed that they all belong to the poorer working class for the most part. Many are down at heel, few have collars, that adornment seems to be taboo. There was the occasional lad from a better family who the writer observed probably took up with a "seamy" gang to annoy his parents and ignore their wishes. He found some of the lads friendly, ready to invite you into a game of banker saying that if you can't play they will teach you. "So the casino of the pavement is busy till the police appear and we all run." This early series on the gangs gave an insight into the psychology of the youthful gangster and the difficulty of weaning him off his ways. One young lad, called Sam, was used as an illustration of how even moving into new, more salubrious surroundings was not a cast iron solution.

Sam it seems had been a "street Arab and gangster down Govan Street way" but he didn't share his family's ambitions. They moved to the leafy suburb of King's Park in the southside where new housing was leaping up in the early thirties and families were making a new start away from the shipyard and slum, enjoying gardens, parks and a nine-hole municipal golf course. Sammy had to move with the family but King's Park was too tame for his taste. Meeting him there he told the writer: "This is an awfu' place. Who could bide here? As sune as I get ma breakfast I gae back to Govan Street and bide tae dinner-time. As sune as I swallow ma dinner I am back to ma corner again and bide tae bedtime." Sammy's nature it was observed could not be changed simply by transportation to a new improved environment.

According to this view of gangsterism most of the trouble was hatched in dance halls and picture houses. Incidentally much was made of the fact that many of the troublemakers were in fact employed – they needed to be to finance trips with a girlfriend to the cinema or a dance hall in the first place. But all this was before the days of the serious wars of such as the Billy Boys and the Norman Conks, and the fights, which seemed often to start over girls or name-calling, were easily broken up by the arrival of the police. At this stage in the evolution of the gangs neither drink nor drugs seemed much of a factor. Occasionally a "rum ration" was taken before "going over the top" but for the most part these youth gangs shunned the pub. The *Evening Citizen* investigative reporter went as far as to say that boozing before battle was exceptional and the gangs are just out for amusement "and being just ordinary modern youths they take the average modern youth's view of intoxicants. They see no amusement or source of entertainment in that direction. Their tendency is to shun it."

Amusement it seems was not confined to the participants in the gang skirmishes. The papers report that when there is a battle between rival gangs, "the public wisely keep indoors to escape stray missiles that are not aimed at them. The people of a district rather enjoy seeing such a fight from their windows. It is good fun for themselves as well as the youths. As soon as the police appear the fight is over and the gangsters run. Then the public are entertained to the delightful spectacle of the big men in blue in hot pursuit of the youths and girls. It is a cheap movie from real life."

This, to the modern eye, seemingly naive series of articles does however give a remarkable insight into the thinking of the time, even if the underlying violence and the way the gangs were to develop over the next few years was hugely underestimated. A delightful spectacle is hardly the right description of what was to follow in the Gorbals and Bridgeton! However the *Citizen* was in white-washing mood. It editorialised:

"To reassure the public in the face of wild rumours prevalent, it should be made clear that the police can break up any gang any time they wish to do so. The policemen on any particular beat make a point of getting the names and addresses of every member of the local gang. This is a very clever piece of work as the gangs will not let the police within a hundred yards of them if they can help it. How it is done is a secret that must not be given away. The result is that, should it ever be found necessary to do so, our police can have every gangster in the city under lock and key within a few hours. So far as the police are concerned the gangster problem is solved."

Maybe they should have let Percy Sillitoe read this before he moved north from Sheffield on his mission to bust the gangs!

Razor-slashing got the same whitewash. The tale was told of an incident when in Crown Street the "cry arose, 'razor-slashers!'" Apparently the alarm rang along the whole street. Pedestrians took to flight, women went into hysterics, police whistles were blown from point to point. The boys in blue quickly reached the scene of the scare to find what was described as "a couple of mites" who by accident had picked up their fathers' razors and carried them into the street.

However the very telling of this tale reflects the real fear of razor-slashing that was around, a fact that seems to have by-passed the reporter. Perhaps he wasn't aware of the case when one young man appeared in court in what was described in the press as "an extraordinary case of razor-slashing". A teenager attacked eight men, all unknown to him, in half an hour. In one case the victim was uninjured but the razor cut through his hat. He caused, in some cases, permanent disfigurement, and the victims were in most cases cut around the face and head. This half-hour career as a razor-slasher started in Sauchiehall Street at 9.45 p.m. and proceeded down George Street into High Street and ended in College Street at 10.15 p.m. The slasher hid his razor in a cap or beret.

Around the same time a twenty-one-year-old was jailed for five years for slashing two men in the Gallowgate. This thug had a weapon made from a piece of wood with razor blades attached to it. He also carried a piece of metal piping as back-up.

Age seemed no barrier to slashing and a case where two boys of ten were each put on probation for cutting another boy and a girl spawned an appeal for the public to take great care when disposing of blades.

The conclusions reached in this series of articles, for all its faults one of the first really comprehensive assessments of gangsterism in the city, are a remarkable mix of naivety, realism and foresight. It was also a forerunner of many undercover operations by writers trying to infiltrate the gangs to find what really made them tick.

The same old complaints echo down the years. For example in the thirties the cry that the police caught the criminals and then were let down by the courts who merely patted a few heads and sent the offenders out on the streets to carry on much as before, was already being heard. The *Citizen* observed that minor offences, if dealt with adequately, may never be repeated, but if dealt with inadequately, inevitably lead on to major ones. It pointed out some flaws in the system at that time. Cases were tried by a bailie "who, as he does not know the law, is himself kept within the law by a legal assessor who he can consult. And as he does not know the ABC of criminal psychology, but is perhaps more concerned about securing votes and preserving his seat for the district from which the offenders may come, merely gives an admonition or imposes a sentence which simply lets the police down. There are young criminals whose career no punishment will check; but there are more whom condign punishment will reform."

The article further added that the old adage about sparing the rod is true of more than children – its principle holds up well in adulthood. The writer called for full-time probationary officers and Police Court Stipendiary Magistrates who would be free to administer the law without "fear or favour".

Then came a plea, still heard with regularity to this day almost seventy-five years on, for classes in the schools on good citizenship. "If we want a generation of citizens who are loyal, upright and law-abiding, we must rear that generation. We must train it from childhood in the principles of good manners, right conduct and loyal citizenship." All this should be taught in the schools. "At present there is no text book on manners, no manual of right conduct, no primer on good citizenship, in our schools. There ought to be such." The school curriculum was said to comprise all subjects except these.

The youngsters were then praised for being a sober generation. This was said to be because the principles of temperance and sobriety were drummed into them by Bands of Hope, Juvenile Temperance Societies, Church Sabbath schools and even the ordinary day schools. The same methods, the writer felt, would be applied to teaching good citizenship. Then in a breathtaking leap of optimism he observed that "if we do thus instruct them definitely and persistently, in the course of one generation our present problem will be solved".

After this came a heavy dose of realism. The difficulty of carrying through plans to open schools as social centres and places where the young could be lectured on good citizenship was highlighted. The gang-types were clearly finished with schools and schoolmasters. The reporter then appeared to torpedo his own optimism with a declaration that it might not even be desirable to have a society in which youngsters didn't form gangs of one sort or another. It was pretty hell-fire stuff: "They will disappear when our youth disappears; when the fire, zeal and love of fun in all youth is suppressed; when to be young is a capital crime; when succeeding generations can be supplied without the irksome stages of childhood and youth; when races appear on the world's stage full-grown from the Creator's hand. The Church and the courts, the priest and the judge, ministers and policemen, may do their utmost to remove and break up our present gangs. But they will only assume another form. Youth ever wishes to be its own leader; to devise its own amusements, to do things for itself. Gangs or no gangs, youths and maidens will consort in groups, rivalry will follow, fights will ensue, weapons available will be used, accidents will happen – and the law will call it crime. So the perennial tale will run."

The final paragraphs soared into the bizarre. "The conclusion that one comes to on investigating and thinking out these problems inherent in the life of big cities is that mankind went off the rails when first they proceeded to build such monstrous excrescences as cities. Let them forsake their cities or burn them and spread themselves out over the habitable globe. But even then we would only be back again amongst our stones, clods and uprooted trees with sore limbs, swollen faces and battered heads".

Sadly this hugely dramatic pessimism was more on target than the early view that a few classes on citizenship would solve the problem! The reference to drinking not being a major problem with the young at that time is interesting and this view seems to be borne out by reports from some of the temperance organisations who despite wanting the demon drink to be banned seemed to find it wasn't a youth problem. In fact the Scottish Temperance Alliance carried out an investigation into the gangs in order to see what part drink played in the mayhem on the streets. Robert Spence reported to them that the gangs were not all modelled on the same plan, or actuated by the same considerations, and that they were not formed for criminal purposes. "The causes of friction seemed to be due, generally, to a religious bias and also due to some gangs having girl members on whose account trouble sometimes arose." He said that it was the general opinion of those who knew the situation that unemployment was the chief cause of the extensiveness of the gang system. Most members of gangs were unemployed, many had never been employed and had no adequate outlet for their energy. "Drinking", he reported, "played little part in the gang life and in no case was it said that alcohol exerted any decisive influence over lives at the present stage."

The opinion was strongly expressed, however, that lack of parental control was often responsible for the mischief into which young men were led and one prevalent cause of the irresponsibility on the part of parents was alcoholism, which therefore became a secondary factor in gang violence.

In the thirties there was almost a rerun of history as clergymen, politicians and others debated in similar fashion to their colleagues in the 1914 to 1918 period on how best to "beat the gangs".

The Second World War brought similar problems on the gang front as had happened in the aftermath of the First World War. During the conflict itself juvenile delinquency figures rose sharply and much of the blame was heaped on the part-time schooling of the era. Fathers were in uniform and at war on land, sea and air and many mothers were doing their bit in munitions factories and other war effort activity. Coupled with this was the fact that part-time schooling had been introduced. Police numbers, always a problem, were also low because of the war. The many clubs and associations who fought to provide alternative attractions for street kids were also hit by manpower shortages caused by the war. Volunteers were in short supply. Clearly the youngsters at risk of turning to crime and gang violence were on a looser rope than at any time for many a year. The effect on crime statistics showed almost immediately. In 1940 crimes committed by children of school age in Glasgow had risen to 3,216 as compared with just over 2,000 cases in 1939. A massive rise. The main crimes were "housebreaking, thefts, gaming, frauds and malicious mischief". The figures, horrendous as they were, gave no indication what percentage were gang-related and what were simply actions of youngsters going off the rails on their own.

Almost a thousand children were fined, 676 were put on probation and 185 were sent to approved schools. In the previous year ten boys had been birched but in 1940 the total was almost a hundred, a huge percentage rise. On publication of these figures the, by now familiar, routine debate on what to do about juvenile delinquency began afresh. The Education Committee of the Corporation said that minor offences were being dealt with by Child Guidance Clinics, closer cooperation was being given by the clinics, and remand homes, probation officials and head teachers were working hard to drum into young heads the importance of care of property and the preventing of wilful damage. The Lord Provost felt the figures showed the importance of discipline in school and the need for full-time education. If schools had been taken over for Civil Defence or national service, other buildings in the vicinity should be used. He rubbished the notion that a school was not a school unless it had around 1,000 pupils.

Crime continued to be a major problem on the home front during the war. And it was not just a teeny crime wave caused by schoolchildren left to their own devices. One of the worst gangs of the war years was the Bath gang, who when some members appeared in court were said to have "terrorised" Anderston district. Four members of this gang were jailed for disorderly conduct and assault on two men in a public house. At their trial the fiscal, Superintendent Fraser, claimed proudly "I have been able to break up this gang". Other members were sent to Borstal and others fined and jailed. The fiscal said that efforts to suppress this gang had not been successful up till this point. And he added that the "only way to keep this gang in a state of subjection was by strong repressive measures being taken by the courts".

Towards the end of war in Europe crime figures took another

spectacular rise. There was also a new phenomenon – hold-ups at gunpoint. On one December Saturday in 1945 there were three such events. Even the Glasgow clippie, famed in the music halls for her "Come oan, get aff" comments, was not safe. A tram shoogling its way down Ballater Street in the Gorbals was boarded by two desperate young men, one of whom pointed a gun at the conductress who came from Govan. They snatched her cash bag and were off the tram and hot footing it into the murky Gorbals closes and backcourts before the passengers could intervene. On the same night a shopkeeper in Keppochhill Road, Springburn was surprised by four men and again one was armed with a gun. In what looks like an imitation of Hollywood films, the shopkeeper's hands and feet were strapped to a chair with insulating tape and the gangsters ransacked the shop, helping themselves to cigarettes, chocolates and the drawings – said to be almost £3! – from the till before they ran out to the street leaving the shopkeeper helpless to raise the alarm. This was a lawless night and in a third raid two young men, again "tooled up" with guns, menaced an eighteen-year-old girl who was in the shop alone and cleaned out the till. This particular robbery took place in full view of a crowd queuing to get into a cinema. No one risked losing their place to go to the aid of the unfortunate lass. If the growth in armed hold-ups had not provided enough action for one night, it was also reported that two men were arrested after a gang fight and a stabbing outside a dance hall in Methven Street, off London Road, in the East End.

During the war when thousands were dying, and parental control was arguably at its weakest, the use of corporal punishment was often in the headlines. The hard liners and the libertarians were frequently in conflict in public. The Chief Constable of Renfrewshire was straightforward in his approach when he spoke as part of a church initiative in *Life and Work* week to an audience of police officers, ministers, teachers, probation officers and welfare workers on youth. His views on birching make chilling reading today: "I have heard many controversies as to whether birching is right or not. Birching as it is done today does not seem to me a good method. I do not say that because I think it is too harsh: I say it because it is not harsh enough.

"I have never seen a child benefit from birching because he found it not to be half as bad as he expected it to be. His attitude was: 'I could take that standin' on ma heid.' Before a birch can be used it must be passed by the sheriff and I do not think it is possible to draw blood with the average birch now in use. If I had my choice I would use a green birch and I would cut them with it: they would not come back to the court again."

One probation officer countered this by saying he disagreed entirely with birching the problem child, but he could think of some parents he would birch.

All this started a war-time stushie on birching that reached all the way up to the House of Commons with words like "savagery" and "sadistic" echoing round the chamber. It emerged that the previous year more than a hundred young offenders had been ordered to be birched in Glasgow. The chief constable who wanted to birch them till they bled was given a sharp reminder by Parliament that "the approval of suitable instruments for punishment is the responsibility of the sheriff not the police". From this distance in time it is hard to comprehend just how vocal and harsh the lobby for birching was. One sheriff told a meeting of the Saltire Society that methods of dealing with young offenders was causing him and others in the legal profession a lot of pain. Punishment sometimes meant detention in quarters "as comfortable as my study". The attitude to young offenders was mealy mouthed and Borstal too "soft". The sheriff even told his audience, "When I was at a public school in England I was thrashed every night – my 'crime' was being Scots – AND IT DID ME A WORLD OF GOOD." Somewhat warped thinking by a man charged with dispensing justice but perhaps a valuable insight into the judgements of the time.

By the end of the war it was the more serious outbreak of criminality seen in the rise of criminals who carried and used guns, rather than juvenile delinquency, that was exercising the authorities. In 1945, there was no argument that Glasgow, like the other major cities in the UK, was experiencing what can only be described by the overworked cliché as yet another crime wave. In these days the Scottish newspapers took little account of the Christmas holidays and there was no break in publication. Indeed as late as the fifties I remember turning up for a newspaper shift as usual on Christmas morning. There was a brief examination of new scarves, leather gloves or a discussion on the latest fashionable aftershave and then it was business as usual. (Not so New Year, however, which Glasgow hacks celebrated with a ferocious energy that left southern colleagues in awe.)

So it was that the newspapers on Boxing Day 1945 focused on the latest crime wave and the comments of Chief Constable Malcolm McCulloch. Housebreaking and robbery with violence had risen markedly, the hold-up at pistol point was something of a regular occurrence. The chief constable acknowledged all this, but claimed that the crime wave was by no means out of control. What Chief Constable ever has!

Crime was on the rise but the percentage of crimes solved was the same as before. He was particularly proud that the CID were solving around 90 per cent of the armed hold-ups. And this was achieved by a force much smaller than it was pre-war. He had a couple of good points to make – urging the authorities to speed up the transfer of police in the services out of khaki uniforms and back into blue. He also wanted the Government to put stricter controls into place on bringing firearms and ammunition into the country. There was no doubt that the war had contributed to the easy availability of pistols and rifles. He wanted an amnesty and for people to be able to hand in illegal weapons without fear of prosecution.

He had to point out that if juvenile delinquency was not rising, it was not going away either and he highlighted a case where two boys of seven or eight were involved in twenty-two house-breakings. Gangs of boys aged fourteen to seventeen were also causing a problem now that the petrol ration saw more cars on the road. The day of the joy-rider had arrived. And stolen cars were also being used for the "removal of plunder" from burglaries. The chief noted that some of the car thefts only moved the car a street or two and were caused by youngsters who would today be called "car daft" indulging in an adventure in driving for the first time. He mentioned that one young joy-rider had fifteen ignition keys in his possession. Mr McCulloch was clear on the causes of this crime wave. As far as youngsters were concerned it was lack of parental control caused by the break-up of family life during the war. The adult crime wave was likewise an effect of the war: "Bands of deserters were roaming the country – men not only from the British services but from the Allied services as well. They were rationless and, if going about in civilian clothes, were men without a means of establishing their identity. Thefts of clothing, of food, of identity cards were the only means by which they could preserve their precious freedom, and their activities accounted for some proportion of the large scale thefts by housebreaking.

"Most of the cases were due to shortage of supplies. So long as there was a ready outlet on the black market, or some form of it, for rationed and couponed goods, there would be rewards for the thief."

A solution would be the lifting of wartime restrictions, but that would take some time. Shopkeepers and householders were urged to make it difficult for the thief. Shopkeepers in particular were warned about the danger of displaying short-supply goods behind thin sheets of glass or on open counters. And, not for the first time in the war against crime in Glasgow, the police pleaded for more help from the citizens. The reluctance of eyewitnesses to appear in court during assault trials is well documented and, given the predilection for violence of many of the hardened gangsters, something that is to a degree understandable. That reluctance was less understandable when crimes other than violence was involved. So the Chief coined a slogan – give the police the tip and leave it up to them. And new technology was brought into the fight. The

Chief wanted the public to use 999 telephone calls to more effect to alert the lawmen on potential crimes. Glasgow was one of the pioneers of two-way wireless telephony as it was called. The police felt the public wasn't well enough aware of the city's distinction in this area, or indeed how successful it was. The nerve centre was a building on Cathkin Braes, a scenic parkland area on the southside not far from Burnside, much used by picnickers and folk escaping the constrictions of streets lined with tenements to take the dog a walk in the countryside where you could look to the horizon and sniff the wild roses along the way. The unobstructed views from this lovely part of the country, 600ft up in the hills yet just a few miles from the city centre, were also ideal for the new police radio communications centre. From the top of the escarpment, a tiring climb on foot from Rutherglen, Croftfoot or Burnside, the views are spectacular, west to the wild Argyll hills, east to the plains towards Midlothian and straight across the city to the Campsies. The police took reporters out to see the site. Linked to the station were forty city police cars (not all in use because of the manpower shortage), the police launch on the river Clyde, police stations and patrol cars in Renfrewshire, Dunbartonshire, Lanarkshire, and through Edinburgh and Dundee to the East of Scotland counties.

Examples of the success of the system in tracking stolen cars and stopping them before they could leave the city were demonstrated. This exercise in educating the public seems to have been a success and the crime wave of the time led to much increased use of the 999 service. Though even almost fifty years ago some folk didn't quite get the concept and there were tales of people calling 999 asking how to join the police.

During this crisis much was made of how weapons brought home as souvenirs were getting into the wrong hands. The problem was much worse than after the First World War when only officers were issued with revolvers. Hence the plea for the amnesty which doesn't seem to have had a great effect. It is interesting that despite the rise in gun-related crime the Chief was on record as being agin the arming of the police since he thought that this would only

Few photographs of the leaders of the major gangs of the Thirties made it into the newspaper archives. In this *Daily Record* shot, Billy Fullerton, leader of the Brigton Billy Boys, has none of the fearsome menace and swagger of his reputation. But the ordinary looking man in a 'bunnet' was an extraordinary figure in the history of crime in Glasgow. In his pomp he commanded hundreds of Billy Boys, a mini-army always ready for bloody battles with rival gangs such as the Norman Conks.

Many commentators of life in the Glasgow slums make the point that it is surprising how few of the children of the denizens of overcrowded tenement homes got into crime rather than how many did! This is a street scene in the Gorbals, Grove Street, in the Sixties and toddlers play on cracked pavements unaware of the attendant dangers of broken shop windows and delivery vans. One little girl has, poignantly, a broken carpet sweeper as a toy.

A backcourt scene in the Gorbals long before the days of yuppiefication, inside toilets and gardens that boast grass. Washhouses, drying 'greens', miniature lakes and a seemingly year-long sea of mud. Appalling housing conditions lasted well into the Sixties. In the late Twenties a government report showed that 13 per cent of Glaswegians lived in single-ends – the highest proportion in the UK. Even in 1976 Glasgow had almost half a million substandard houses and there were almost 50,000 families on the waiting list. The conditions in Gorbals were often mirrored in other areas like Bridgeton, the Calton and Finnieston.

Above: A room and kitchen in The Dwellings, Green Street, Bridgeton, in the early Thirties. Annie Knox is beside her gleaming fireplace, the centre of tenement life and usually the matriarch's pride and joy, and her son Ernest sleeps on a couch.

Left: The legendary Chief Constable Percy Sillitoe, known as 'the Captain' to his loyal force, did much to curb the pre-war gangs with a policy of meeting force with force, and the ability to use police 'intelligence reports' to good effect. His elite squad of specially recruited police anti-gang fighters nicknamed the 'untouchables' were lawmen as tough as the hardest neds spawned by the Glasgow slums. And often a good deal smarter!

Gorbals Cross as it looked just after the Second World War. The tram rails still criss-cross cobbled streets and in an unlikely juxtaposition a florist is sandwiched between Doyle's Bar and a restaurant. Now, in a multi-million pound regeneration scheme, a few hundred yards to the south of the cross, lie state of the art modern low-rise flats providing an attractive place to live for a new generation.

20 8 75   B

SCRO   1122.

NORVAL   WA

Walter Norval is generally accepted to be the first of the modern era of Glasgow Godfathers. A wily lawbreaker he saw the advantages of several criminal enterprises linking up under his leadership. But the law caught up with him and he was jailed for armed robberies on a bank and a hospital payroll. Interestingly, drugs were not a feature of his reign as Godfather and indeed in later life he railed against them.

The weapons used by the gangs were, and are, numerous, inventive and always horrific. For a time the easily hidden open razor was the weapon of choice, but when gangs went to war there was little limit on what could be turned into a weapon. Here a plain clothes detective carries a haul of weapons dropped by fleeing gang members . . . in this case a crowbar, hatchet, bottles and belt. Other gang weapons included bicycle chains (with or without the added refinement of steel spikes welded on), machetes, hammers, and long lengths of rope with heavy bolts at the end, used in the style of the South American bolas.

Few photographs exist of actual gang fights of the Thirties. The sheer scale of the battles is a surprise to many commentators today. Glasgow Green was a regular venue for blood letting between gangs squabbling over territory or sectarian beliefs. Rutherglen Bridge was another area where the gang members clashed in their hundreds. This is Tollcross Road in 1933 with women and children, as well as decent hardworking men in collar and tie, fleeing in terror as gangsters battle it out.

One-to-one battles often took place to establish leadership of a gang. The leader of a 'team' had often to be prepared to fight off rivals for the top spot. The strongest took the spoils and the infamous 'Glasgow kiss' (a head butt in the face of an opponent) was often a feature. But as this photograph shows fighting in the street was always a dirty business, even if no weapons were involved. A good kicking of a downed opponent was deemed to be tactics. The rules of gangland have not changed down the years.

Graffiti is a fact of life in Glasgow city centre almost as much as the schemes. The curse of the spray painter has resisted all attempts to curb it. Mindless morons take pleasure in defacing their surroundings with slogans.

Arthur Thompson Snr, seen here in his prime, liked in latter years to pose as a 'retired business man', the pin stripe, smart shirt and tie, almost a uniform. But for years this fearsome career criminal ran the east end crime scene and grew wealthy on the profits. An associate of the big London mobs, including the Krays, he survived gangland assassination attempts and died in his bed of natural causes in 1993.

Young Arthur Thompson was a criminal of a different stripe, without his father's fearsome persona or the ability to cash in on being handed the family business. Nicknamed the 'Fat Boy' or the 'Mars Bar' kid, he ended up in Peterhead Prison on drug charges. Remarkably his father had never been handed down any long stretches. Young Arthur was on a release trip home to the east end from jail in 1991 when he was gunned down in the street in what was presumed to be a gangland killing. No one has ever been convicted of his murder.

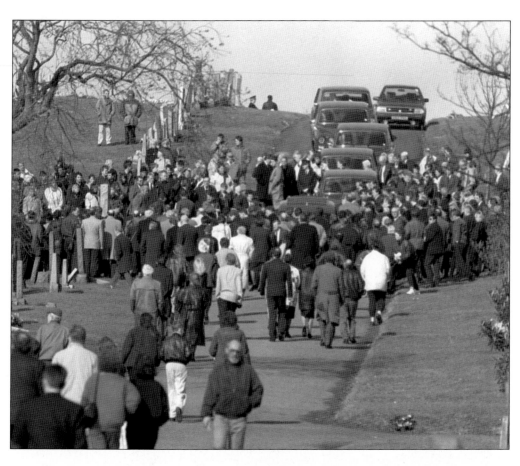

For a man who styled himself as a business man, Arthur Thompson Snr had a funeral that would have done a Mafia don proud. There was a procession of funeral cars, florists had a field day and neatly dressed men lined the streets to pay their respects. There was a police guard at the cemetery and even a bomb scare which turned out to be false. The old Godfather was laid to rest beside young Arthur.

The controversial Easterhouse project in 1968, when Frankie Vaughan and local politicians got together to try to stop gang wars in the scheme. To some the project was seen as currying favour with wild and turbulent youths who deserved punishment rather than a youth club. A feature of the project was an amnesty on arms negotiated with some help from the then Prime Minister Harold Wilson. Here some youngsters gawp at the weapons which have been dumped in bins on waste ground.

Liverpudlian song and dance man Frankie Vaughan was audacious enough to do something about it when he read, while appearing at the old Alhambra Theatre, of the troubles in Easterhouse. A hard worker with the Association of Boys Clubs he set about trying to stop the fighting and find other outlets for youthful energy. Here he is on a return visit to the scheme in 1977.

Thomas McGraw, aka The Licensee, was once part of the Thompson empire before setting off on his own account. He is said to have built an empire worth around £10m and spends his time between 'business interests' in Tenerife and Glasgow.

Thomas 'TC' Campbell, was, along with Joseph Steele, convicted of the ice cream wars murders, but both have declared themselves to be innocent and have fought, down the years, to clear themselves. They are currently out of jail on interim liberty pending an appeal.

Paul Ferris, the man cleared of killing young Arthur Thompson leaving Frankland Prison in Durham in January 2002 after serving a sentence for gun running. Like Tam McGraw he was once a member of the Thompson team and, if nothing else, his old mentor's taste for sharp clothing seems to have rubbed off on him.

make matters worse and end up with the police dealing with more and more armed offenders: "The task of the police is to disarm other people." London was also going through a similar crime wave and there the top Scotland Yard men were also blaming the war years when might was right and the law of the jungle prevailed, stamping a get-rich-quick philosophy on many of the populace and spawning that almost comic figure of the time, the spiv who could always get you what you wanted. Even if you didn't have the coupons. Bombing, rationing and the black market had all left their mark on the people. This attitude was carried over by some to civilian life and the shortages and the ability to easily dispose of stolen goods was fuelling the country-wide crime wave.

7

"WE'RE NO WANTIN' ANY O' YER PING PONG"

A study of the history of attempts to curb gang and youth crime could bring you to the dispiriting conclusion that much of the well meaning "do goodery" chronicled down the years has turned out to be largely ineffective. Today's gangs are very different from those spawned in the stinking slums early in the last century. The grinding poverty often thought to be the anvil of evil in the bad old days has been ameliorated if not removed. No one in Glasgow now lives the nightmare of unhygienic outside lavatories or of shared stair head toilets. No one is denied the chance of a good education. And unemployment is lower than for many years. Education, education, education is a god to the politicians. Even if they often fail to deliver.

Many of the forces that drove street crime in the past have been removed. The growth in drug usage is, of course, a major new factor, though it is naive to think that drug misuse, and the battle for control of supply and profits, is a purely modern phenomenon.

Followers of the crime writing genre will be familiar with Conan Doyle's Sherlock Holmes injecting himself with cocaine as a sort of intellectual leisure pursuit. His habit puts the legendary detective into something of the same category as the arrogant coke-sniffing young highfliers of the international money markets or the cheap glamour of soap opera stars, risking the destruction of their noses.

But the fact remains that despite the massive changes in society the gangs are still with us.

Down the years Glasgow has had a succession of "gang busters", a phrase much favoured in newspaper headlines. Clearly the gangs, despite some remarkable successes, just can't be said to be "bust".

But the forces of good have won many a battle. There is no denying that the most famous "gang buster" of all, Sir Percy Sillitoe, did cut crime with his strong arm methods which would be politically incorrect these days. He met force with force, added some innovative police thinking with regard to intelligence reports, and mobility for his specially selected tough anti-gang squads of policemen. And met with success. Likewise Lord Carmont took on the razor-slashers with his policy of long jail terms for the slashers and stabbers brought before him by the police.

And, as we have seen earlier in this book, as far back as 1916 there was a groundswell of popular opinion that what was needed was more activities for youth, more social intervention to keep them busy and out of trouble. The sort of thinking that brought such as the Easterhouse Project has been mirrored down the years by other attempts to tackle the gang problem at its roots rather than simply deal with its effect. And even the most mean-spirited critics of do-goodery are forced to admit that intervention and a bit of social engineering and religious input has had periods of success. The gangs may have continued to exist and do so to this day but how many young men and women were weaned away from them by enterprises like the Easterhouse Project?

Glasgow has a long history of men of the cloth getting involved in trying to sort out the troubled youngsters who were the breeding ground of gangs. In Easterhouse itself, to be discussed in more detail later, names like Ron Fergusson and Peter Youngson, and Bill Christman, an American-born Church of Scotland minister who became its first full-time prison chaplain, spring to mind as ministers who rolled up their sleeves and did their bit to clean up their patch. Father Willy Slavin and Father Jim Lawlor were also much involved with the youngsters who found themselves on the wrong side of the law and doing a stretch in the Bar-L.

Two of the earliest men of the cloth to plough such difficult furrows were the Rev. J.A.C. Murray and the Rev. S.H.R. Warnes who planned to tackle the east end gangs with ideas reminiscent of those of the Easterhouse Project.

Their initiative took place against the background of Drygate gangs' battles and a warning given by Lord Alness at a sitting of the High Court in 1930 that time might come when "use would have to be made of the lash and to revive an old statute of George IV, under which the penalty of death could be imposed on those who went razor-slashing".

The Church of Scotland was much concerned about what was going on and Mr Murray of Park Church and Mr Warnes of St-Francis-in-the-East in Bridgeton thought the answer was to provide "recreational facilities and to substitute games for fights". Mr Murray told an evening meeting of the presbytery, called to discuss the reform of non-churchgoing youths in the east end, about the uneasiness in the city about what was going on with the gangs. He said that by a succession of remarkable coincidences recently the paths of himself and Mr Warnes had been drawn together. They made an investigation and found that within a radius of 150 or 200 yards of Mr Warnes' church there were no fewer than ten or eleven gangs with a membership of 250 to 300 boys and men, closely organised and ranging in age from fifteen to more than forty.

The two ministers made in the first instance what they called a very timid approach to these gangs. They met quite a welcome. Mr Warnes was able to conduct a party to Hillfoot for an afternoon's football, there was an invitation to a dance, and another to go on a ramble. They found that each of the "bands", as they called them, had territory and a name. They found them well organised not just for discipline but to control finance.

Mr Murray told the presbytery that he considered the gang to be a phenomenon directly thrown up by the reaction of young life in the east end to the depressed conditions of their time – "the economic conditions which had crowded them together in such unsanitary areas and which had produced for them an unemployment market in which there was little or no demand for their services".

Not for the first time someone who really knew what was going on in the slums remarked that it was surprising that the problem was not worse than it was.

Murray and Warnes seized on the notion that the gang rivalry element could be turned to good use. They wanted to give it an outlet in activities such as football and boxing and gym work. They also identified the gangs' gregarious instincts as a source of hope, something that could be moulded into team spirit. A third admirable characteristic was independence of spirit.

This showed itself when the ministers made "a very cautious feeler" about the cost of running a football league. No problem said the lads. They would charge a penny at the gate and cover all expenses. When a ramble was organised tickets would be printed and sold to pay for the trip into the country.

It is intriguing to note that even this early in the battle against the gangs a *Glasgow Herald* leader in praise of the enterprise could remark that it was no new idea! It went on to observe that a boy who enjoyed kicking shins would probably enjoy kicking a football. And in a realistic addendum it was pointed out that "the roving bands of boys whom they seek to discipline, by sport and comradeship, have not grown up in a day and there is more than a day's work in their reform". It warned of disappointment ahead. Apparently "the extravagant public notice that has been taken of the gangs in some quarters will not be easy to subdue". But overall the idea was welcome.

And it did get off the ground and a few months later the papers were able to report the formation of a street-corner football league in Bridgeton. The new organisation was called the Rockcliffe Parish Football League and was said to embrace eight teams of young men from the corners that lie between Bridgeton Cross and Main Street. Games were played on a vacant piece of ground near Shawfield Park on Wednesday nights and Saturday afternoons. A Captain Weyman of the Playing Fields Association was appointed secretary and Bailie Alexander Munro of Dalmarnock ward was one of a group of honorary presidents. Incidentally in these pre-television days there were many public meetings to discuss the way forward, often held in church halls and the like. One lady who did some public speaking in favour of providing facilities for the young was wont to recall an amusing court case to show that the gangs were certainly not unintelligent. She liked to recount an occasion when a gang carefully chose the smallest member, hid him in true Trojan horse style in a tea box and smuggled him into a tobacconist's shop to await closing time and in the wee small hours open the doors for his friends.

The street-corner leagues were a modest start for the Kirk, but later on and for many years the Churches leagues were to become a mainstay of amateur football.

Another early precursor of the Easterhouse Project was the association of boys' clubs which grew up in the Gorbals. And the 1950s saw the emergence of a remarkable Church of Scotland minister, walking in the footsteps of Warnes and Murray, who was labelled, a tad optimistically in retrospect, by the old *Evening Citizen* as "The Man Who *Really* Broke the Glasgow Gangs".

This was the Rev. J. Cameron Peddie, who had been minister of Hutchesontown Parish Church in the heart of the Gorbals for around thirty years. His story was told in the *Citizen* in January 1955.

His series was introduced to the readers by another remarkable Church of Scotland minister Duncan Campbell, who was responsible for the paper's extensive coverage of church matters.

This was at a time when Lord Beaverbrook, the wealthy Canadian who owned the paper – and whose father had been a minister of the Kirk – took a great personal interest in church affairs in Scotland and made sure the Glasgow evening paper reflected the goings-on of the Kirk in exceptional detail.

Duncan was a busy man but took time off from his ecclesiastical beat – and the Beaver's "no bishops in the Kirk" campaign – to introduce the crime series.

Like all good hacks the minister-turned-journalist began his article with an eye-catching paragraph or two:

"Alarming scenes in Crown Street when three gangs came into conflict were described in court when four youths appeared charged with being members of a gang known as the 'Southside Stickers', that they did form part of a riotous mob of evil-disposed persons.

" 'The shopkeepers live in a state of terror,' said a witness. 'I saw one of the accused leading a crowd of about fifty young men. He was brandishing a stick, cursing and swearing and shouting. The melee lasted about twenty minutes.' "

This scene took place in the early forties and the newspaper report saw it as symptomatic of the Glasgow of that era when "citizens were afraid to walk the streets alone after dark and beaten-up shop keepers refused to talk". A combination of years of depression and the city's squalid slums had led to the law of the jungle operating in the poorer quarters, vicious gang fights broke out on the slightest provocation – a jilted girl or the result of a football match. According to this report all over the world the word Gorbals made people shudder and conjure up a picture of violence.

With masterly understatement the writer remarked that "Glasgow had a bad name".

The *"really"* in the title of the series came from the fact that, according to Duncan Campbell, when Percy Sillitoe arrived in Glasgow to do battle with the gangs, after success in a war on the neds in Sheffield, his job had been made easy for him: "Not by a strong-arm man, not by any counter violence but by a quiet young man with an Aberdeenshire accent who not so many years before had won bursaries to Gordon's college and Aberdeen University to study for the ministry."

The Reverend Peddie had started his ministry in central Scotland with a post in Barrhead but had become intrigued by the newspaper tales of slums, crime and gang warfare. Could he do anything about it, wondered this man of God.

So he went to the Gorbals where he didn't find life as black as it had been painted. His congregation was made up of friendly decent folk making the best of battling against poverty and deprivation. And he found much evidence of the legendary friendliness of the folk in close and street that surfaces so often in the many Gorbals memoirs.

But this remarkable minister went to work on the bad guys as well. He spent a holiday trying to get to know and gain the confidence of the hard men on his patch. And he came to the conclusion, like many before him, that many of the gang merchants who terrorised the innocent were little more than "mischievous youths with no legitimate outlet for their high spirits" and who, with time on their hands, were turning to violence and crime.

In that area of the city he found that the gang hatred didn't have a religious basis. The two main gangs, the Southside Stickers and their sworn enemies the Liberty Boys, were each composed of both Catholics and Protestants.

J. Cameron Peddie swiftly realised that more than conventional church clubs would be needed if he was to make any difference to the culture of violence in the young. This conclusion was underlined when a group of wild youngsters, when asked to join church clubs, rejoined with: "We're no wantin' any o' yer ping pong". So a new approach was tried – give the potential troublemakers clubs of their own in which they entertained themselves and ran it on their own account. Thirty clubs with around 4,000 members came into being and each club had an honorary leader – the Rev J. Cameron Peddie. It was an enterprise not without danger yet the minister, despite verbal threats, was never attacked.

Such close contact with violent youngsters was reported not to have adversely affected the minister's view of the world. According to Duncan Campbell, twenty-five years after starting his clubs J. Cameron Peddie was still a believer in his fellow men and there was no trace of toughness or cynicism in his make-up.

But clearly he was a man unafraid to tackle the gangs head-on. He tells of trying to find out who the Southside Stickers really were. It wasn't an easy task. On a street corner he met eight boys who confessed to being members of the Stickers. Ready to start one of his unconventional clubs he approached them with the idea of a non-political non-sectarian club with their own committee to run it. Asked for their names and addresses they gave false ones and failed to turn up for a meeting. Mr Peddie took to the streets to find them. Several of the original group he approached were said to be "on holiday", a euphemism for jail. What are you up to? asked the minister, and he was told the Stickers were out for vengeance after the Liberty Boys had done some serious harm to one of their boys. The group was asked to come along to the Kirk vestry for a chat and they agreed. Cameron Peddie tells a remarkable tale of this meeting. About forty turned up and they had an assortment of weapons, one lad had a huge iron sword, others jemmies and razors. Cameron Peddie must have been a brilliant negotiator for there was no gang fight that night and even the boy with the sword was in favour of asking the Liberty Boys to join the club to be formed. That was a bit too soon, but a start had been made in ending bitter enmity. Incidentally once the clubs had been up and running for a time many of the lads presented their weapons to Cameron Peddie as souvenirs.

Special smoker concerts were held with fish and chip suppers. There were sing songs, boxing and dancing. Local people were generous with gifts of equipment, and the press, the police and the council were helpful. The clubs had a syllabus printed and main principles were brotherhood and good citizenship. Drinking, betting and bad language were banned. One important rule was that in all disputes the leader's decision was final. Peddie tells of many meetings in the vestry to discuss matters and after they were over the youngsters told him of their experiences at the various "holiday resorts" – as they described them – of Polmont or Saughton. Barlinnie was their place of rest, refreshment and entertainment. Sixty days there was as good as three months "doon the watter" they told J. Cameron Peddie. Peddie was of the opinion that one of the reasons for youths coming out the better for a spell in jail was the food, rest and regular hours, something mostly not on offer on the outside.

The parish minister's negotiating skills were often in demand. Once he effected a reconciliation between a youngster who had been jailed for killing a man in a gang fight and a man who had given evidence against him. And when Mike and Bob finally shook hands after long discussion Cameron Peddie could write: "I talked to them in what I imagined the founder of our religion would have said in similar circumstances. Thus the man who had killed and the man whose evidence had condemned him were reconciled. It was a thrilling moment for me."

Peddie's skills even extended to working with the police. There was gloom in the Stickers' club one Friday night. There was a big game the next day and their star player was in the cells. At the request of the minister the police released him for the match which the Stickers duly won. Then he returned to the cells and his case was dealt with on the Monday. Cameron Peddie always resisted attempts by the police to recruit him as an informer – the boys were his friends and he was not going to spy on them.

The boys, too, had a strong code of "honour" which seems to be a worldwide gang phenomenon. Peddie wrote: "The first thing that impressed me deeply about the boys was their amazing loyalty to their class. Supposing I asked them, someone is killed in a fight and one of your men, though innocent, is charged with the death and you know the guilty man to be one of the other gang, would you not save your own man by giving away the guilty person? 'No,' they replied. 'If you are to mix with us, sir, you must understand we never give anyone away, even an enemy. This is the first principle in our code of honour.'"

Peddie went on to remark: "I was profoundly impressed with this and though I did not swear allegiance to this attitude to the law, I resolved not to let them down. I never gave away any of them and they knew it. What a magnificent spirit they had if only turned to other channels."

The reference to deaths in fights was not a remote possibility.

The *Citizen* series was illustrated with a fearsome collection of photographs of weapons including a cosh filled with lead and covered with wire barbs and bicycle chains with wire barbs woven into the links.

The concept of the club away from the church grew and the Stickers soon had hundreds of members and premises in a disused factory which happened to be in the territory regarded as theirs by the Liberty Boys who would shout through the windows "Come on out and fight you minister's boys". Cameron Peddie managed on one occasion to stop the Liberty Boys armed with picks and spades battling with the Stickers. A brave as well as a good man, he patrolled the streets to 4 a.m. that night to stop any more trouble breaking out. This was the sort of behaviour that won respect and soon the Boys had their own club, honorary leader J. Cameron Peddie. Other clubs started included the Wellington, the Benthall, the Harmony, the Clydesdale and the Premier.

Peddie never preached religion to them and indeed some of the Kirk members weren't too happy about any meetings in their halls, but he claims the clubs brought many families into the Kirk. This truly remarkable figure said that the only preaching he permitted himself was to urge the lads to be true to their faiths whether they were Protestants, Roman Catholics or Jews.

All this may not have stopped gang warfare in the Gorbals but it did diminish it. Peddie started various schemes to provide employment for the lads; one called the Lightning Distributing Agency took handbills and samples from door to door. There was also a firewood business which had limited success. Interestingly labouring was often not an option to club members – most of them were "underfed, pinched and stunted in growth and just didn't have the necessary physique".

The influence of J. Cameron Peddie went much further afield than the Stickers and the Liberties: no less a figure than King Bill Fullerton is on record as saying he made even the Billy Boys see sense.

Two other men played a major role in curbing other gangs in the forties – a legendary youth welfare worker Major Malcolm Speirs and a Barlinnie governor Mr R.M.L. Walkinshaw.

Speirs was the star in an odd incident in Billy Fullerton's life. Speirs gave the gang leader something of a beating, perhaps the first time Fullerton had taken his medicine without raising a fist in retaliation. It happened after the King of the Billy Boys had been collared by the police after a fight in Dalmarnock Road and taken to the Eastern police station. Fullerton met Speirs in the detectives' room and was told that if he agreed to take his punishment he would not have to surrender his bail.

Fullerton agreed and met the bold major in his Buchanan Street office. Using a clothes brush Speirs administered a spanking that hurt physically, but even more mentally. Fullerton later told reporters he remembered this incident more clearly than others where he was attacked with lethal weapons.

Walkinshaw had a big effect on Fullerton as well. The Billy Boys' frequent visits to the Bar-L let them know each other well. Fullerton liked the governor's attitude to two prisoners fighting. He would tell the warders to stand back and let the battlers finish their argument and that way no resentment was allowed to fester.

Walkinshaw died in a train accident and his obituary noted that "He cooperated wholeheartedly with the prisoners' help societies in every effort to reform the prisoners and give them a chance of becoming respectable and useful citizens. He took a broad humanitarian view of his duties . . ."

Just as all this effort to provide a positive reaction to the gangs was reaching some degree of fruition, along came the Second World War. Many of the Billy Boys and the Conks and all the rest went off to a different sort of war. Some as soldiers, others in the Royal and Merchant Navies, some in the Air Force. Many served well, they were natural fighters. Many never returned.

And after the war the informal association of boys clubs faded out of existence. Now in the twenty-first century there is still violence on the streets of Glasgow as there is in most similar cities. Arguments about who bust the gangs, if it ever happened, is futile.

But there is no argument that Christian visionaries like J. Cameron Peddie did nothing but good and prevented much gang violence. That battle to keep idle hands from evil work goes on today.

8

EXPERIMENT IN EASTERHOUSE

In the fifties and sixties memories of the war began to recede and people were starting to enjoy a better lifestyle. But there seemed to be no end to the recurrent cycles of crime wave, period of calm, crime wave. It was as if the newspapers and commentators kept the phrase in a mental drawer ready to be pulled out and used again and again.

It surfaced with particular reference to the east end post-war scheme of Easterhouse in the late sixties. There was a more than usually violent outbreak of gang activity in the housing scheme, a classic Glasgow "outer circle" estate where thousands of folk had been decanted from inner city slums to bright new housing in areas with no recreational facilities for young or old. The bleakness of such places is hard to imagine for those who have not experienced it. The streets in such schemes tend to be long and featureless, the windows of flats offering no heart lifting views of greenery or countryside, merely endless vistas of rubbish-strewn pavements. The cheeriest sound is the chimes of the occasional ice cream van – though in Glasgow even these vans were often selling more than lemonade and ice cream to folk desperate to ease the pain of their existence. Children looked in vain for play parks or games fields. The open areas left to them by accident rather than design, often at the end of one street and the beginning of another, were littered with old furniture, broken bottles, waste paper. And shops provided soon became mini-fortresses, the windows boarded up or covered in graffiti-splashed corrugated iron as defence against the frequent attacks. The sheer dispiriting feel of such an area was remarkable. At times the whole scheme felt soaked in a despair that affected visitors as well as residents. These were the areas society seemed to have forgotten. Easterhouse had, however, a visitor, from Liverpool of all places, who although shocked by what he saw and heard talking to locals, young and old, was not paralysed into acceptance of the status quo by the surroundings. This was at the height of warfare between teenage gangs in the scheme. He decided to do something about it.

The unlikely visitor was one of Britain's top entertainers, Frankie Vaughan, a song and dance man who was playing the old Alhambra. This was in the days before TV killed stage variety, and the headlines in the Glasgow papers caught the attention of the touring troubadour. With the help of others, local politicians, ministers and folk who just felt something had to be done about the mess the place was in, he helped start what was to become known as the Easterhouse Project. This blatantly obviously well-meaning move was not without its critics. The Glasgow head-in-the-sand attitude surfaced again and there were claims that highlighting the problems to the world just made things worse. Shades of the thinking of decades ago. There was also some legitimate concern about glorifying gang leaders. What was to become a massive project started in a simple way with the singer trying to exercise his fame by asking the gangs to meet him and attempt together to settle their differences. The flak started to fly on day one when an eminent lawyer Lionel H. Daiches Q.C. said: "Many young people would love to meet Frankie Vaughan and have their photograph taken with him. Young thugs frequently made the headlines but there was no publicity for decent living youths." But the lawyer did concede that there was much to commend the proposal of a meeting to settle differences provided the victims of gang assaults were also asked to attend.

But the meeting went ahead as planned and Vaughan told the press that he had been assured that four Glasgow gangs would lay down their arms – swords, bayonets, sledge hammers and meat cleavers. The leaders of the Drummie, Pak, Rebels and Toi told the singer they would leave their weapons on neutral ground opposite St Benedict's Hall in the heart of Easterhouse as a first step in ending gang warfare in the area. Frankie in turn told them he would help them set up a club or centre of their own. This "peace in our time" agreement came after eight hours of cloak and dagger operations to ensure the meeting, arranged by local social workers, took place in private. The entertainer said: "We must stop the violence and I have told the lads that I will take nothing to do with them unless this is done. I will stand up for them against anyone and will come up here anytime they feel they need me – but the main part of the work is up to them."

A youth who took part in the talks and called himself Gerry said: "We think Frankie speaks our language better than anyone. We will lay down our weapons – but we would like the police to stay away for an hour on Saturday night. We don't want to get nicked on the way to neutral ground." Incidentally, Gerry was quoted, remarkably, as saying "we don't use bicycle chains because we think they are square." After that plea to the police he said they could come along and pick up the weapons. He added: "Most of the gangs don't want to fight. We will tell those that want to keep on carrying weapons that they can't run with us and its our territory."

The planned club was to be built by the boys with help and was to be unconventional, though if they needed any assistance the Boys' Clubs of Great Britain, something the singer was also involved in, would lend a hand. A fundraising dance was proposed and the senior magistrate Frank McElhone promised the use of a hall.

Initially the police would not agree to the method of disarming. But there was no stopping Frankie Vaughan – he sought the help of the then prime minister Harold Wilson. He telegrammed Westminster: "Yesterday I went to Glasgow and persuaded leaders of feuding gangs to end the bloodshed. They agreed to turn their weapons in on Saturday evening to a spot where we will build a youth centre. Have just been told the police will not agree to a one-hour armistice. Results of this could be disastrous, even tragic. I appeal to you to intervene and let our peace efforts continue unhindered."

Wilson replied that he understood the Scottish Office had been in touch with Chief Constable Sir James Robertson and heard he would agree to the proposed surrender. Ever the wily politico, Wilson added that the conditions the chief constable required were a matter of police operations "in which I cannot intervene". But the log jam had been broken and there seems to have been an outbreak of common sense. Suddenly all was palsy-walsy as the gangs might say. Frankie Vaughan commented that he agreed with the chief constable's proposals for supervision and said he appreciated the legal position. The Lord Advocate issued a statement saying that so far as he was concerned he regretted that he did not think that it would be in the public interest for him to be involved in the picturesque arrangements reported to have been proposed by the young men mentioned in the press. Any arrangement to which he gave cognisance would necessarily have to be carried out under police supervision. He wouldn't have been a lawyer without a talent for pomposity!

The statement went on to say that if there were people possessed of such weapons whose sole concern was to get rid of them, there should be no difficulty. "They can get rid of them in various ways, it does not matter how, provided there is no danger of them falling into the hands of potential lawbreakers." The chief constable said he was prepared to cooperate along the lines suggested by the Lord Advocate and that any person wishing to dispose of an offensive weapon should wrap it in paper, securely tied, and hand it in to any police station. No names or addresses would be taken. And with a nod in the direction of the original proposal he said: "Any person wishing to dispose of an offensive weapon in the Easterhouse area may take it wrapped in paper to the vacant ground opposite St Benedict's school between 7 p.m. and 8 p.m. on Saturday night where disposal and collection will be under police

105

supervision. If these conditions are strictly observed the police will not intervene." The entertainer who was appearing in Birmingham said he was delighted at the PM's telegram. "It is only right that the police be on hand when the boys lay down the weapons. If the police were not there they could be picked up by other youngsters and the whole plan wrecked. The police will be there not to watch the boys but to collect the weapons. Much has been done to bend the law and I think the boys will not let me down." Norman Buchan, Parliamentary Undersecretary of State at the Scottish Office appealed for the public to stay away and give the experiment a chance.

All this was front page news in Glasgow's papers, and not just in the tabloids, and the twists and turns in the saga were reported in depth and daily.

The actual hand-over opposite St Benedict's was deemed to be a success, though the city-wide appeal for a hand-over at police stations only got a couple of responses. A crowd of about 200 watched opposite the school and there were press and TV photographers galore – even a crew from NBC in America. Around a hundred weapons were carried to the spare ground by a combination of gang members and youth leaders who carried weapons for those "too shy" to hand over in public. In a lovely Glasgow touch local traders took advantage of the event – there were four ice cream vans and two fish and chip vans present. Any way you can turn a dollar . . .

On the Monday a *Herald* leader made the pertinent point that if a life had been saved or an attack forestalled by Frankie Vaughan's decision to get embroiled in the politics of gangs in Glasgow then it was a notable achievement "for which both the leading and ordinary citizens of Glasgow will be grateful".

One leading citizen who did not see it quite that way was Bailie James Anderson, the police convener who had been agin the experiment from day one. He had a violent disagreement with Frankie Vaughan on the BBC television programme *24 Hours*, describing the amnesty as a publicity stunt. He said the affair had tended to create hero worship and publicity and to glamorise the gangs. He claimed some of the gang leaders had told him they were only going along for the publicity ride. He claimed that on the very night of amnesty there was a gang fight where twenty young hoodlums chased five other gang members and stoned a bus. Vaughan replied he had investigated this "supposed gang fight" and that there had been no injuries. This was lively television and the argument soon cut to the old one of crime and punishment in general. Both sides of the coin were given a real old hammering. The police convener spoke his mind: "I believe that we simply have to meet violence with marked violence. It is simply as brutal as this. I don't like saying it but this is what I believe . . . The greatest deterrent to a person committing a crime is the sure and certain knowledge that they will be caught and convicted and adequately punished." He went on to praise harsh sentencing. From the libertarian corner the entertainer responded: "The reason for the fighting is because of the conditions these kids, these children, live in. They are not men, they are children. I know for a fact that if I lived there with my family my children would run around with these kids and be involved in these gang fights. Parents in this area have the choice to keep the kids indoors or let them out and they may be involved with a gang. If you are not going to give these kids a chance to rehabilitate themselves you are calling kids of eleven, twelve and thirteen criminals." The incident crystallised much of the dispute over the Easterhouse experiment and indeed it had echoes of the arguments, discussed in earlier chapters, that were going on even during the First World War about how to deal with gang violence. The opponents of the initiative were not pleased when the singer chartered a plane to take gang leaders to a meeting he had organised in Blackpool where he was appearing and, coincidentally, where Frank McElhone was holidaying, the Lancashire resort being then as now a great favourite with Glaswegians. There were other promising moves: the chief constable agreed to be a trustee for the club that was to be formed and even Bailie Anderson moderated his stance, if only marginally.

He wanted the boys to help remove the ugly graffiti that was scrawled on almost every available wall before he would consider an invite to be a trustee. Help in this was to come from a character famous in Glasgow folklore as the man who cleared the menace of the starlings from George Square. Before stone cleaning specialist John Cameron was hired to tackle the plague of the birds, huge flocks gathered at dusk over the city centre square bombing buildings and pedestrians alike in something that resembled a horror scene from Hitchcock's *The Birds*.

Cameron was a master of more than the starlings. He was also an expert in graffiti removal and he was asked to help. Any success in this area, a matter of great concern to Bailie Anderson, was however sadly short-lived as a visit to most of Glasgow's schemes today will confirm.

The boys lobbed in a few other names as potential trustees, including comedian Jimmy Logan and Celtic star Stevie Chalmers. And boxing legend Peter Keenan offered to help in a similar experiment in Drumchapel where he had family. It was a time of optimism in the battle against gangs and teenage crimes. Inevitably some of it was misplaced.

Two of the youngsters who had flown to Blackpool for the controversial meetings ended up in court at the end of August in 1968, only a few months after the initiative had started to grab headlines. They were put on probation for three years after a plea by one of Glasgow's best remembered legal eagles, newspaperman turned lawyer, Bill Dunlop. Bill told the court that this was the most important case he had ever been entrusted with, because of what might happen to the tremendous efforts being made by Frankie Vaughan and the Rev. Peter Youngson of Easterhouse, and others, to rescue and make into decent citizens people like his client, a lad called McKenzie. Bill Dunlop said that "When he came out of the approved school he was still leader of the Drummy gang but he was sick to death of the greatness that had been thrust upon him and wanted desperately to turn away from gang activities.

"As the leader of these youths, seventy or eighty of them, McKenzie had been closely connected with the chief constable, Mr Vaughan and Mr Youngson in this wonderful project which will mean that these youths will be kept off the streets, will have a decent centre with a swimming pool and all the advantages they deserve."

Incidentally legal families seem to be something of a Glasgow institution; Bill's son is a respected legal figure as a sheriff in my part of the country, Kintyre. Gangs may not be a feature of that area, but there is nonetheless much work to be done in Campbeltown Sheriff Court. And Martin Smith, who on occasion acted with the Great Defender, aka Joe Beltrami, for the Thompson family, had a father who was also a well known city lawyer. There are other examples that prompt the thought that though brawling may be in the blood of too many Glaswegians, others seem to carry the genes that lead to legal robes.

In the Easterhouse case Mr Youngson gave evidence on behalf of McKenzie and another accused called Begbie – they had been involved in an assault that took place before the project started – and he told the sheriff: "I am far from being starry eyed about gangs in Easterhouse, after serving seven years there." He went on to praise the two for their efforts to bring peace to the scheme and saying that they had "gone into alien territories in Easterhouse to test the amnesty".

All this brought an interesting response from the Sheriff-substitute N.D. McLeod: "Over the years, in dealing with cases like yours, I have become aware of the tensions that have built up between groups of young people, all citizens of Glasgow, coming from the same homes, with the same hopes and difficulties, who yet regard themselves as sufficiently different to consider each other as enemies. This tension between gangs must have become nearly intolerable for members. I have been told that this is the position of at least two of you (McKenzie and Begbie).

"I am well aware that people, not only in Easterhouse, but elsewhere in the city, have become increasingly more alarmed and resentful of your behaviour and that the parents of most of you are sickened and worried by this behaviour."

He added: "I will thrust you upon our already over-burdened probation service and ask the probation officers to bear in mind the special possibilities of this case." The optimism was reaching even to the courts.

The newspaper coverage went beyond day-to-day reportage on the unfolding events and the polarisation of attitudes spawned by the project. There were many in-depth features and analyses of the problem of the gangs. A reading of some of these features would make a healthy diet for those today who have difficulty with the size of the problem. A special series in the *Herald* for example. A paper, as I well know, that puts accuracy and considered language at a premium and shuns the sensational. However it could still declaim that "however much one may deplore the showmanship and publicity associated with the flights to Blackpool and so on, most thinking adults are bewildered by the wave of gang terrorism, the suborning of witnesses, the extortion of protection money, and the stabbing of innocent passers-by in the main thoroughfares of the city, the gangs are a fact of life".

The writer went on to express dismay at the negative attitude of Bailie Anderson and the Corporation. This analysis picked up on a theme expounded by many quoted in this book . . . the contrast between a life lived in monotony, drabness and a sense of hopelessness and the false excitement of gang life.

The old argument on what sort of clubs or organisation could woo youth away from the gangs was rehearsed yet again in depth. The Scouts and the Boys Brigade were deemed too respectable to have much influence, a rather harsh judgment because both organisations had success in giving worth to individual lives. But down the years it has been shown that attempts to "reform" youths from the outside can be self-defeating. The trick seems to be in getting the youngsters involved in running the "clubs" themselves. J. Cameron Peddie would agree.

The *Herald* underlined this point with a report from Birmingham where problems similar to that of Easterhouse were faced. And articles which used to have bold headlines like "How to beat the gangs" were no longer so confident, but now ended with a question mark.

The Bishop of Birmingham had much success with a club called the Double Zero in 1965, transforming "leather jacketed Rockers who used to be the scourge of the Midlands from Hell's Angels into angels of mercy". The club was said to have the usual facilities ... coffee bar with pin-ball and football machines, table tennis and snooker, dances and midnight movies and outings to motor racing circuits like Oulton Park. But there were innovative practical policies like an emergency service run by members to take blood or drugs from hospital to hospital, and there were also members who would provide motorcycle escorts for ambulances in fog. The key was participation, and the members ran the club in democratic fashion. Easterhouse youths went south to study the Birmingham operation. The *Herald* writer who did his own investigation, David Kemp, was impressed but pointed out that Birmingham and Glasgow are very different. "The English city does not have Glasgow's tradition of violence and religious friction while Glasgow has no immigration problem on the Birmingham scale. Nevertheless in attempting to rebuild the communications bridge with the disaffected and alienated young, Birmingham is launching an experiment which cities like Glasgow must study closely. By failing to provide adequately for youths growing up in the deserts of its great housing schemes, Glasgow sowed the wind and is now reaping the whirlwind. But there are signs now that events springing from the Easterhouse amnesty could mark an important turning point." National Service and its benefits or otherwise was also an issue at the time. The newspaper commentators were by now more cautious and all the false dawns of "gang busting" hung heavily on the city's history. There was a realisation that even in Easterhouse an amnesty would in time only lead to a "phase two" arms war and that progress, if it was to be made, would be slow and progressive. There was no magic bullet, as it were, to defeat gang culture.

Some observers blamed much of the problem on the quick fix to urban deprivation by building multi-storey flats. A generation was growing up in homes which denied youngsters freedom in their first five years or so, the fate of babies born into the upper blocks of a high flat. Mothers cannot let a child out to play safely when they are isolated from a play place, relatives or neighbours and when the only practical means of exit is via a lift that a pre-school child can't operate. The local authorities were urged to have a close look at what the planners had done and one critic stated that the barren housing estates were more packed with the risk of moral degeneration than were the overcrowded slums of the past. It is a point well made, for in a graffiti-smeared high rise flat, corridors stinking of urine and stale air, and with little chance of social intercourse with neighbours, community spirit was hard to grow. There are many who looking back at the black days of the old tenements acknowledge that they, surprisingly, produced both a spirit of community and friendship between neighbours who lived in each other's pockets. A modern high flat was a lonely place for a young mother struggling against poverty to raise a good family. National Service had the disadvantage of militarism but the advantage of discipline for many who had never experienced it. One commentator said that: "There are many things that will not be made available except by the hands and time of young men doing National Service. With proper leave, proper pay, proper living conditions, proper discipline and proper targets to aim at, the youth who has failed to make the grade unaided can be helped to fit himself into society." In the language of the day he added: "Experience shows that nearly everyone appreciates belonging to a worthwhile show."

It was acknowledged that most of the trouble came from youngsters who had grown up in homes where there were no effective attempts to encourage standards which any society will accept. National Service was seen as something of a substitute for that, but it was also acknowledged that there needed to be life after a couple of years in the Army or RAF. Jobs to allow newly found skills to be exercised were a priority.

One leader-writer of the day thundered that unless the lack of proper parental guidance was addressed, successive generations would grow up impinging on the rights of others and that "all must rally round if the story of unrelieved gloom of mass municipal housing is not to be the story of a series of lost generations". Words that have resonance today.

The Easterhouse Project had early success that was not sustained at the same level down the years, but it was for a long time a major influence on the young in the scheme though the fact is that there are still youth gangs in the area in the twenty-first century. But Frankie Vaughan took the sneering criticism of folk who should have known better on the chin and fought long and hard with local leaders and the more far-sighted politicians in the area to produce something that was well worthwhile and which down the years kept many a young person out of the clutches of gang life. A sort of stocktaking of the success of the project came naturally in 1982 when one of the key figures left after seven years. Constable John Nolan was a remarkable police officer who ran the project in the Westerhouse Road Nissen Hut centre. The *Evening Times* called him "a banjo playing pied piper figure". He reluctantly left his patch to go to Boston, Massachusetts, with his newly wed American-born wife. He had plenty to say before catching the plane: "Easterhouse folk have a distinct sense of humour and they need it." The humour evinced itself in the nickname for the hut centre – the Bears' Disco. "Why not?" he laughed. "After all it is the 'bears' who attend. Or, at least, they were when I first got involved here.

"We even have the 'Wee Bears' Disco' for the five- to twelve-year-olds, and nobody complained about the title. It is a personal joke, and something they can identify with." Constable Nolan did not wear rose-coloured spectacles and acknowledged that in such a vast housing scheme there were many parts the project could not reach. "But in the seven years I have been here, I hope I can say that three areas, in which previously there was a great deal of bitterness between rival factions, it has ceased to exist. It has been a long hard slog, and is by no means over yet. But we are getting there. We now have all three local groups together. No longer do the locals resent our presence. At first many were thinking that if the project wasn't here, they wouldn't have to put up with trouble on their doorstep. A different attitude has developed." Glasgow has always been fortunate to have policemen, such as John Nolan, with a deep interest in police community involvement. He had worked in the notorious Blackhill area and run a youth club there, so when he was offered the chance of a full-time secondment to the Easterhouse Project he jumped at the chance. On leaving he received a special presentation from Sir James Robertson who had bent a few rules to help establish the project. That Easterhouse humour surfaced again. "Here's another wee laugh. It is a cheese and wine soirée but the bears will be along later." Frankie Vaughan sent a letter, too. Constable Nolan left some interesting comments and advice for his colleagues involved in such initiatives. "Things did not happen overnight. The first task was to keep the rivals apart until they got to know each other. Separate discos at first then introducing indoor sports in the afternoons and gradually bring them closer together in outdoor activities.

"This is what produced the most profound change in them. It's funny but the further away they were from Glasgow the better. We went and still go camping, rock climbing, canoeing, windsurfing, hill walking, sailing, mountaineering and every activity has a full programme geared to keep everyone occupied during the day and out of pubs." Strathclyde Police went on record with a deserved tribute to the PC's tremendous work.

But such initiatives seem to have some sort of inbuilt shelf life, running out of steam somewhere along the way, even if they continue to keep going, and there are many examples of this in the history of Glasgow gangs.

However, history records that to some extent the Easterhouse Project was an experiment that worked. Thirty-two years after it began, papers, part of a study undertaken by Glasgow University's

School of Social Studies into gang activity in the city, were released in January 2000 showing that during the Project's heyday crime in the scheme had dropped significantly.

This official accolade which put the carping of the critics into proportion came too late to give succour to the singer who suffered many health problems in later life. He died following heart surgery in September 1999. But his name lives on in Easterhouse and Glasgow folklore. A star who had risen from humble beginnings in a Liverpool slum left his mark on a troubled Glasgow housing estate.

At the time of his death local councillor Jim Coleman told the press: "Frankie Vaughan will always be remembered by the people of Easterhouse. The Easterhouse Project is still doing good work and will serve as a tribute to his memory."

Other memories of the years spanned by the Easterhouse Project are not so welcome. "It is not the Tiber, it is the Clyde in Glasgow which is foaming with blood," claimed Thomas Galbraith, the Conservative member for Hillhead in the Commons in May 1968. This over-the-top comment came in a debate on the Scottish Office's handling of what was described as the latest crime wave. (As I have noted, crime waves have rocked the city with depressing regularity from the days of the Penny Mob to Paul Ferris.) Galbraith wasn't alone. Surprising as it may seem to the political observer of these days, Pollok (pre-Tommy Sheridan and his headline-grabbing firebrand socialism) had a Tory MP, Esmond Wright, who said the city was "a crime laboratory" and called for a Royal Commission to investigate the causes of crime.

All this was part of a swirl of right-wing reaction to the problems of the late sixties. Bailie James Anderson who was so cynical about the Frankie Vaughan initiative got himself into another fine lather when a petrol company offered steak knives in a sales promotion scheme, seemingly oblivious to the fact that dozens of shops, including some with fancy addresses and elite customers, had such implements on general sale, or perhaps more accurately available for shop lifting. And Progressive councillor John Young of Cathcart criticised Frank McElhone for his offer to meet with gang members on their own ground. Mr Young showed that the singer was not the only man who could showboat by accusing him of wishing to play the role of Eliot Ness. It was a time of high political emotions. John Young advocated more parental control and the return of the birch rather than "irresponsible suggestions to negotiate with juvenile gangsters". Never a man to mince words Bailie Anderson favoured a suggestion that there should be sentences of twenty to thirty years for serious crimes of violence and added that the only place he would be pleased to meet those who had committed violent crimes would be as a member of a visiting committee to Peterhead Prison to make sure they are not mollycoddled. (An unlikely happening in a jail renowned for a tough regime.)

This was followed by ringing declarations that the honeymoon was over for the thugs. The Bailie wanted a ten per cent increase in the rates to pay for a war on crime and reorganised the meetings of the police committee. There was to be one meeting a fortnight instead of five to allow members to concentrate on the fight against violence and "it would be left to officials to handle such matters as ordering fodder for police horses". But the honeymoon was far from over and the marriage of deprivation and crime was to continue as strongly as ever.

There are no quick fixes to the problems of teenage crime and over the years the same medicine keeps on being prescribed with, sad to say, indifferent success. Bailie Frank McElhone, in between spats with Bailie Anderson, proposed at this time an idea that was something of a return to the ideas of the Kirk's pioneering ministers Murray and Warnes in the east end so many years ago – football coaching for the youths who were drifting into gang violence. He wanted the help of big name footballers from Rangers and Celtic to coach lads and suggested that many of the city's junior football grounds were underused and could be a weapon in the fight. "Just think of the thrill they would get if Billy McNeill and John Greig came along to give free coaching."

But, sadly, neither the sixties' rhetoric of the right nor the well-meaning intervention of the left was truly successful.

9

THE GODFATHERS

Nothing shows the changing face of gangland in Glasgow better than the rise of the Godfather. In the early days the leader of the gang was almost always the man who was the strongest, most ruthless, bravest and best street fighter. Skill with fists, pickaxe and broken bottle was the hallmark of a gangland general, and they led by example.

The fearsome reputation of such as Peter Williamson of the Beehive gang, discussed in a previous chapter, was such that it was said that only a couple of other men in the Gorbals could give him a run for his money in one-to-one battle. Billy Fullerton of the Billy Boys and Bull Bowman of the Conks were, when in their pomp, fearsome individuals who could use their fists to quell rebellious foot soldiers as well as tackle their enemies.

Similarly the gangs of the First World War and before were led by individuals who had the physical presence to emerge as the leader of the pack.

In fact sociologists worldwide who have studied gangs and leadership do seem to come to something of a standard conclusion that the leader is usually the most disturbed and violent and the one with the lowest impulse control. Though, as in most science, you can always find a dissenting voice or different theory. But the popular conception, fuelled by Hollywood movies on the Mafia and television series galore, of the toughest going to the top and ruling by fear and violence seems to be as correct in Glasgow as in Sicily, Chicago or St Paul. An ability to outwit the forces of law and order, even if that means simply having the intelligence to cooperate with the best lawyers, is also a factor in major gangs.

Some sociologists divide gangs into three types – youngsters with time on their hands who enjoy their own company and build a relationship, others who operate against the law primarily for profit, and yet others who simply enjoy violence.

Glasgow has all three. And a goodly number of variations on the theme. But it was only in the seventies that the concept of organised crime in the conventional sense crept on to the scene. The activities of Walter Norval, generally recognised as Glasgow's first Godfather of crime, are much different from those of a previous era, but no less violent.

Norval (in later life he became Walter Norville) was a neat fit for the stereotype gang leader, well able to control his troops with his fists. He also had a vain streak, and liked to dress in what he assumed to be some style. Polished shoes and pin strips seem to go with the territory. There is an amusing story of the American Mafia which underlines the danger of a dress code. A group of US mobsters, more than fifty of the top bananas of organised crime, once gathered, indiscreetly, for a pow wow at the mansion of Joe Barbara in a woody hamlet in upstate New York. The vast number of out-of-town plates on squadrons of limos attracted the attention of the locals and the police were tipped off. A raid ensued with the Mafiosi scampering for safety in the woods. Most were promptly arrested, easy to spot as the guys with the shiny pointed shoes deep in the leafy woodland.

Norval's vanity extended to more than his dress: he had the habit of continually combing his hair in such a fashion that it disguised an ear disfigured in some brawl or other. His career in crime made an unforgettable mark on the city when in 1977 the High Court in Glasgow was petrol bombed overnight just before he and others were to stand trial for armed robberies.

The petrol bombs had rained into the court through a skylight and the obvious intention was to destroy articles to be used in evidence at the trial. But the incriminating material was undamaged, safe in the basement from the burning petrol. Until the court received a £5 million facelift twenty-three years later in 2000 you could still see the fire-damaged and blackened wood in places, a grim reminder that, cornered and in trouble, a Glasgow gangster is a dangerous animal.

Norval's daughter – described by reporters as attractive and raven-haired – was cleared of the bombing and intimidating witnesses but her husband was jailed for five years. The authorities were determined that the trial would go ahead and there was only a few days' delay until the south court which was not so badly damaged was patched up and put into use.

The police had been aware of the danger of intimidation and during the trial that lasted sixteen days there were remarkable scenes. There was speculation that the trial judges, Lords Cowie and Kissen, might be attacked in some way and they were escorted to and from an exclusive club in the city centre where they were staying. The club itself was under guard. The High Court in Saltmarket took on the appearance of a fortress with armed guards all around and swarming over adjacent buildings. The four prosecuting counsels were also guarded for the period of the trial. Witnesses, too, were deemed to be at risk. They were brought to the court in secure vans in the company of armed detectives, used back doors, and were whisked away to secret addresses when they had given evidence.

The public benches were cleared and anyone going near the steps of the court had to prove their identity. Every morning crowds of workers going about their business had the diversion of watching a convoy of police cars and vans, sirens wailing, and with an armed support unit in attendance, making its way to the court.

In the end Norval was jailed for fourteen years for armed robberies on a hospital payroll and a bank. These raids resulted in thirteen men appearing in four separate trials with six being acquitted and seven – including Norval – getting a total of seventy-four years in jail.

Norval liked to think of himself as Glasgow's Al Capone, and it was a claim not without foundation. He was the Mister Big of that whole operation. But unlike Big Al, who went to a long stretch in Alcatraz for the mundane offence of tax evasion, Walter Norval had ended his infamous criminal career in a spectacular trial unlikely to be forgotten or repeated in the city.

A well-built and strong man he had in the early days taken the classic route to gangland leader by eliminating rivals with coshes and knuckle dusters. But his era produced a new phenomenon in the story of the gangs. Leadership of one gang was not enough for Norval and the mindless battles of the old days when bicycle chains and bottles flew at rival gangs often for no other reason than they were there, was not attractive.

In the manner of his idols in Chicago, New York and St Paul, he and his boys began to make forced amalgamations with other gangs.

And when they were "organised" to his satisfaction he became the mastermind behind a string of robberies bringing in tens of thousands of pounds. In their book *Such Bad Company*, George Forbes and Paddy Meehan say that on occasion he took part to show that he was still a force to be reckoned with but for the most part he contented himself with selecting targets and planning with military precision. And, of course, claiming the lion's share of the loot.

His fame in the underworld and his flash – he liked the sweet life of big cigars, top of the range cars, and big-name label champagne – helped him recruit young thugs, mostly it is said from Milton and Govan. These young Turks handled most of the violence necessary but they knew that to step out of line was dangerous.

Norval was well in funds from his early robberies and he was known to be a generous payer for info on where payrolls would be delivered, on opportunities to breach bank security and other nuggets of intelligence. The grapevine cost him much cash to keep it healthy but it was worth it in terms of rich pickings. Norval was said to plan in great detail and he had patience. Every aspect of casing the joint was gone into. Where to hide the getaway cars. Just when to strike. Escape routes were researched and dummy runs made. Gang members even went as far as to disguise themselves as workmen to study potential targets.

In his role as Mister Big he had the patience to go through all this for months if necessary and the power to control the impatience of his gang members.

In the best traditions of crime films he even rehearsed with his followers what would happen in a bank when they broke in. How to get the cash with speed and brutality became part of the rehearsal. There were to be no surprises when the Norval mob swung into action. It was all painstakingly thought out. It was also said that he had a secret arsenal, a garage in which he kept all the weapons necessary for his associates to carry out their criminal enterprises – masks and gloves, revolvers, shotguns, hammers, axes and knives.

But his taste for the flash was to be his downfall. Inevitably the police began to take note of such a character with so much money and not much visible support.

There were some surprises when they began to investigate. The gangster who was fond of health clubs and saunas and as much *dolce vita* as you could find in Glasgow in these days lived in a council house in Milton. Unlike his successor Arthur Thompson with his huge Ponderosa H.Q., known to everyone in the city, Norval's expensive tastes didn't seem to run to property. And he was married with seven children and six grandchildren. However he did have a glamorous blonde mistress in the wealthy avenues of the West End, something that did not seem to worry his wife overmuch.

Like many another Glasgow hood he had the brass neck to collect unemployment benefit and any other social security hand-outs going. Even Arthur Thompson would do this!

Norval also helped his elderly mother collect rents from flats she owned. Presumably his reputation on the streets made it a singularly bad idea to fall behind with the payments. But while Norval, a betting man, was busy in the bookies in the afternoon and the casino in the evening, the police were building up a dossier on him. The similarity of method used in various robberies pointed to a mastermind who was an expert planner. And the more the detectives looked at Norval the more they became convinced he was the man.

He had one lucky escape. He took part in a breakfast-time raid on a van delivering wages to a hospital. The cops quickly realised this had all the hallmarks of a Norval heist and rushed to raid his home.

The bold boy had arrived home only minutes before them but quickly undressed and appeared soaking wet in a bathrobe claiming he had just got up and knew nothing of any raid on a wages van. His wife confirmed this fanciful tale. And shortly afterwards he went on holiday to Tenerife with his mistress.

All seemed well on his return when he collected some insurance money on the death of his stepfather Joe "the Pole" Kotarba. Kotarba, according to Meehan and Forbes, ran a vice ring and was stabbed by a pimp trying to take over the operation.

After yet another robbery with his style written all over it, the Serious Crime Squad paid another visit. Norval had to switch off the television racing coverage and go down to the station for questioning.

But Norval shrugged off his wealth as a product of his gambling and he assured the cops that weapons found in his luxury car must have been planted there by his enemies. The police didn't buy such arrogant nonsense and after they had put some heat on his acquaintances one of them cracked and began to sing like the proverbial canary, ensuring Norval was on the way to a stretch behind bars.

The witness who did so much to put Norval away was a much younger man, Philip Henry, who had been a favourite of the old gang leader and Norval was very angry with himself for misjudging the character of a lieutenant. Such was his rage about this let-down that Norval is alleged to have ordered the younger man to be killed. But for now Norval was caged and the big time robberies and raids were over.

My book *Glasgow's Hard Men* tells of an intriguing postscript to the Norval years. In June 1999, Norval, now known as Norville, hobbled from Glasgow Sheriff Court virtually unnoticed after admitting possessing cannabis worth £15. The Crown had accepted his plea of not guilty to being concerned in the supply of amphetamine. His defence lawyer told the court that the elderly man before them "was acutely embarrassed about being connected with drugs". The accused was very anti-drugs and said to be helping on a voluntary basis with a drug rehabilitation programme in the city. The lawyer said Norville had once made "banner headlines" (and how!) but now lived a quiet life as a great grandfather. He suffered a lot of pain from arthritis and was on medication and found that cannabis was a great pain reliever. The quiet man left court accompanied by a few friends. Perhaps his extended family of grandchildren was the reason for his disquiet at the spread of drugs and the crimes committed over them. His successors as Glasgow Godfathers have no such squeamishness, indeed drug dealing and control of supply is now the major cause of gang violence on the streets.

It is depressing how often a single battle victory against the gangs is historically seen as winning the war. Even such experienced readers of the crime scene as George Forbes and Paddy Meehan fall into the trap. In their book they point out that with the Norval saga over, no organised mob stepped into the void.

They say: "Nor is it likely that there will be heirs to the criminal throne. With the redevelopment of the inner city involving the lessening of the population by a third during the late sixties and seventies, with the destruction of close communities, the chances of another underworld network like the Norval system has lessened. While Norval was running his empire, the city still had the remnants of a cohesive underworld where organisations could be set up on an integrated basis. Now with the break up of the inner city areas, it has meant the police have scored a clinching victory and ended the danger of organised crime on a large scale."

It may have looked that way at the time but history was to prove yet again that gangs are hard to bust. Before long new organisations were to form and people like Paul Ferris and the Thompsons, Senior and Junior, were to show in dramatic bloody fashion that victory over Norval's clever scheming was only a single milestone on a long, long journey.

In one sense this assessment was correct. Post-Norval the major gangs took on a more territorial look with different factions controlling different areas. The lesser, mostly youth oriented, gangs which were spawned on the street corners, had always tended to operate in tight local fiefdoms. This type of gang still runs in suburbs and inner city alike, but Norval's organisation was only the first of similar collections of heavies. Though after him the driving force was control of drugs.

Interestingly his most infamous successor Arthur Thompson Snr built up a fearsome organisation on protection, money lending and extortion before in its latter days moving into the drug business. Anyone with the slightest interest in crime in Glasgow acknowledges that for a time at least he was the unchallenged Godfather. Like his transatlantic counterparts Gotti and Joe Bananas, he died of natural causes – a heart attack in his case – despite a life lived in the spotlight of violence. His funeral on March 18, 1993, was a gangland occasion not to be forgotten.

The old mobster was buried under police guard in Riddrie Cemetery in a family plot, alongside his murdered son Arthur Jnr and his daughter Margaret. Uniformed police officers cordoned off the cemetery, just behind the Thompson redoubt of the Ponderosa in Provanmill Road. Bomb disposal experts were called to the scene. The alarm was a hoax, but an army bomb disposal unit travelled from Redford Barracks in Edinburgh and there was a controlled explosion. The bomb alert had begun after the police received an anonymous tip-off about a suspicious device. The police refused to let strangers into the graveyard which lies on the edge of the notorious Blackhill housing scheme. The Thompsons had serious enemies and the police were taking no chances. House owners nearby were wakened by the explosion and the police activity. During the actual funeral plain-clothes and uniformed police mingled with the mourners who were around 500 in number.

As the hearse stopped alongside the family plot, four giant wreathes were removed to reveal an ornate coffin. The flowers formed the words: "Darling, Papa, Arthur and Pal". The service was conducted by the Reverend Russell McLarty, of St Paul's in Provanmill. He said that the Thompson children, Billy and Tracy, wanted their father remembered as a kind and generous man, who loved life and took great pleasure from his family and grandchildren. He added: "Arthur Thompson should also be remembered as a man of dignity who was loved by many people." The widow, Henrietta, was comforted by her surviving son Billy.

According to the *Evening Times* mourners had travelled from many parts of Britain to attend. They were said to represent a wide selection of the friends and associates he had made in "the criminal, business and professional community".

It was a send-off that would have satisfied a Mafia Don. Traffic police were drafted in to control the tailbacks of up to three miles on the roads in and out of Provanmill and hundreds of wreathes and floral tributes were left at the graveside. One was believed to have been sent by the notorious English gangsters the Kray twins, said to be friends of the deceased. As was, it was claimed, former London heavy, Mad Frankie Fraser. Actually there was a degree of cooperation between London heavies and those in Glasgow in the heyday of Arthur Snr. It was often said that Thompson sent footsoldiers south to work with the London gangs and broaden their experience as it were. There is a tale that when in the south some of the Glasgow hard men had to be dissuaded from being too hard – dead men don't pay extortion money. There was even a touch of violence on the day of the funeral: newspaper photographers were jostled by mourners and had coins thrown at them.

All this show must have been hard to take for the police who had spent so many years working to control the Thompson empire. Old Arthur in his later years, he was 62 when he died, had made a great play of being simply a "retired business man" and indulging in a taste for smart suits, polished shoes and neat shirts. When alive the newspapers took him on at their peril. Arthur had powerful and usually successful legal representation. To protect his "just-a-business-man" routine he sued an Edinburgh paper which had the nerve and cheek to link him to the underworld – and won. Half the settlement was given to Radio Clyde's Cash for Kids campaign. His bulky figure was well known around town, attending sporting and charity dinners and the like. Anyone who met him did not take long to sniff out the scent of aggression, danger and power that drifted off him till his death. To his son, Arthur Jnr, he may have passed on a desire to be a gang leader, but, as in many a legitimate business, a successful succession was to prove far from automatic. Young Arthur was not of the same stamp as his father.

After the death of the old man the police were rightfully fearful of what would happen next. One senior police officer predicted: "There could be bloody warfare out there. There is an empire of dough to be fought over and there are a lot of neds desperate to get their hands on it. Then all hell could break loose. We will be watching closely."

It was a prescient observation. There are some who say that the violence in the streets of Glasgow even in the year 2002 has it roots back in the squabble over the break-up of the Thompson empire.

Arthur Snr, though dying relatively young, had had something of a charmed life considering the business he was in. He had enemies galore. Indeed before that heart attack took him out of the gangland game he had survived at least two assassination attempts. His wife's mother had died in an attempt on Arthur's life in 1966 when their car was blown apart. And twenty years later another attempt was made on his life when he was shot in a city bar.

Taken to hospital he refused to cooperate with the police on nailing his attacker, in a sort of tartan version of the Mafia culture of Omerta. With some wit, considering all this, he like to tell reporters that "I have more friends than Hitler had an army." Maybe, but there were heavy enemies, too. Another attempt on his life had failed in 1990 when he broke a leg when pinned up against a fence by a car. His was a violent life.

Arthur Snr had ruled the crime scene in Glasgow, and particularly the east end, for many years with only short times behind bars. But not too long after young Arthur became actively involved in the family empire he ended up behind bars doing eleven years for drug dealing. That he would take up a life of crime was totally predictable; after all it was the family business. Sadly equally predictable was the fact that he was unlikely to be successful. Overweight and podgy he had none of the presence of his father. Worse he had a fatal flaw for a would-be gangland leader – he talked too much. Known as the Fat Boy, or the Mars Bar Kid, he was desperate to earn some status and respect from the east end Glasgow hard men who had filled the Ponderosa, and its many rooms, furnished with little regard to cost and even less to taste, during his formative years.

But even before the doors of Peterhead clanked firmly behind him he was written off as a loser by many of his drug scene rivals. In prison in Peterhead a visiting *Herald* journalist found him deriving some odd satisfaction that he was in a tough prison, surrounded by tough men. It gave him momentarily a little of the status he craved, but the hard men caged alongside him didn't rate him.

The prison visit for journalists took place in 1989, not long after Peterhead had seen some violent rioting. And the prisoners were allowed access to the press and young Arthur used this concession to whinge about his so-called innocence and rave on about the corruption of the police and the complicity of the press in his downfall. He even complained that when speaking to the then Prisons Director Mr Peter McKinley, the official did not seem to understand he was speaking to intelligent men, not gas meter bandits. The irony of this was that the real hard-tickets in Peterhead thought of Arthur himself as little more than a gas-meter bandit! At the end of the press visit a prisoner made a remark that turned out to have remarkable foresight. Referring to the podgy wannabee gang leader he opined that "That slavering bastard should shut up because he is safe in here. He will not survive a day outside."

Pretty accurate. The Fat Boy was soon to die in a hail of gunfire. From Peterhead he was moved to Noranside Prison in Angus, without much in the way of walls or barbed wire, where the inmates were supposed to be exposed to the civilising influences of agriculture deep in the heart of the Scottish countryside. Six weeks after entering Noranside young Arthur would get the chance of a first home leave. Judging by the remarks of his fellow Peterhead inmate, taking that visit was taking a risk. For while he was languishing behind bars he was trying to pull strings in the drug trade back in the east end. His enemies, the men who had moved in when he was taken off the scene, didn't like that. New arrangements had been made. They could do without the Fat Boy messing around on the patch. But maybe young Arthur just couldn't read the signs or maybe he felt he had to take the home visit or lose face. Whatever the reason he sealed his own fate by stepping outside Noranside and heading home to Provanmill and for him the rare treat of a meal in a good Glasgow curry house and a reunion with family and gang associates.

A man who had known him well had told reporters that if "he had half a brain he could have taken over Glasgow's crime scene". But that didn't happen and his antenna was not sharp enough to pick up the warning signs and stay a little longer in the rural tranquillity of Angus. For one reason or another the pull of the east end was too strong.

The end for the "Fat Boy" came suddenly and violently shortly before midnight on August 17, 1991.

No doubt that many a night in the grim cells of Peterhead, Shotts, or even in the less arduous surroundings of Noranside, young Arthur had longed for the taste of an authentic curry with all the accompaniments, in the city labelled, by those who know, the curry capital of Britain. So it was that the home visit led, almost before it had started, to a visit in the company of his common-law wife Catherine to a city centre Indian restaurant. It was to be a gangland last supper.

The long-awaited meal over, young Arthur drove to his parents' home no doubt for an important chat without the prison screws overlooking and overhearing what was going on. But the talk took only a few minutes and Arthur Jnr decided to walk the short distance to his own home. Another mistake. Three shots rang out over Provanmill Road. Two .22 bullets thudded into his back, a third grazed his cheek. One of the bullets that had entered his back penetrated through to the heart. The Fat Boy was standing and there was no sign of blood but the wound would prove mortal. His sister Tracy heard the shots and ran out from her home to hear her brother reportedly gasp: "I have been shot, hen. I am going to collapse." He was then lifted into his brother's car and taken to the Royal Infirmary whose outpatient department has legendary skill and long practice in patching up east end villains on a Saturday night or Sunday morning. But young Arthur was beyond medical help and died within the hour.

This was an event that stirred up some considerable heat in the criminal community. Who would pick up the pieces of the Thompson empire, who had the audacity to take out the heir to old Arthur?

The first was less of a mystery than the second. To this day no one knows for sure who pulled the trigger that fateful night in Provanmill Road. The man who stood trial for the killing was John Paul Ferris, a one-time friend of the Thompsons and a much feared figure in gangland. He was alleged to have acted with Bobby Glover and Joe "Bananas" Hanlon in the killing. This evil duo had been found dead in a blue Ford Orion on the morning of the funeral of young Arthur, killings orchestrated with Mafia-style timing to make a statement to the underworld. The discovery of the bodies started an extraordinary spell of police activity in the east end. The police were well aware that the power vacuum after the death of the Fat Boy would spawn many a low-life battle and they were intent on pre-empting further trouble. A day of action began with a raid on two homes in Provanmill and ended with what the papers called a "forthright statement of intent from the force's most senior detectives". The families and friends of Glover and Hanlon were roundly criticised for failing to cooperate with the investigation. Instead according to CID officers they were "choosing to deal with things themselves".

The police made a breakfast-time raid on Thompson's home armed with search warrants. A police helicopter noisily chopped the murky skies above as dozens of heavily armed officers, some with dogs, others protected by shields, entered the house. A few yards down the road another posse of similarly armed men entered the house of Arthur Thompson Senior. The entire street was sealed off for more than three hours. Officers carrying handguns took cover against a wall as others carried out a detailed search of both homes. The police justified such massive armed presence on the streets by claiming that it was needed because of intelligence reports they had received.

It was a truly dramatic episode in the battle against the drug dealing gangs – some officers entered the houses with crow bars and sledgehammers. And several members of the Thompson family were kept cooling their heels in a parked police van as the search proceeded. By mid-morning Arthur Snr's other son Billy was taken away, voluntarily they said, by officers. And the law also took possession of a white Vauxhall Astra from the premises. All this prompted the legendary lawyer Joe Beltrami, aka "The Sage of West Nile Street" and "The Great Defender", to thunder out in his famous ringing tones that he had been instructed by the Thompson family to make a complaint to the chief constable "regarding certain aspects of the police operation today". Incidentally Joe had a long association with old Arthur, representing him on many occasions in an "excellent business relationship" that lasted more than thirty years. Joe disliked the term Godfather almost as much as Thompson and he was quoted as saying: "People always claimed that he was in charge of organised crime in Glasgow, but I never accepted that. Arthur used to scoff at the term Godfather and make a point of getting me to take action when the media used it." It was a viewpoint that wasn't shared by many senior police officers. However the famous lawyer's complaints on this occasion helped to provoke a police response. Senior officers called a news conference to emphasise to the public that every resource necessary would be used to complete the inquiry.

The officer responsible for CID specialist services, including criminal intelligence, Detective Chief Superintendent John Fleming, described the current spate of violence as the product of "an ongoing feud between regional factions". He said: "The drugs trade in Glasgow is controlled by major toughened criminals. Very often they resort to acts of extreme violence to protect what they consider to be their jurisdiction and they strongly resent anyone trying to muscle in on their scene." He told the conference that these criminals had no hesitation in arming themselves with guns and warned there could be further deaths resulting from this serious spat between the gangs. He added: "However these targets know themselves who the targets are and 99.9 per cent of the population is safe as long as they keep to their present methods." Mr Fleming was in an extremely frank mood and he went on to say that police information indicated that certain people's lives were in danger. "In the past we have warned them about the potential danger but they continually choose to flout any suggestion of protecting themselves or getting out of the scene they are in." He indicated that the potential victims themselves knew who was a risk and revealed that he had personally warned Hanlon and Glover that their lives were in danger. He said: "I told them a year ago: 'Unless you get out of this scene then the next time I see you will be in the mortuary'." The hoods' response to such frank and accurate talking was to tell the detective to get on his bike. Mr Fleming also confirmed that Arthur Thompson Snr – remarkably described by the police in his own favoured words as a Glasgow business man – was also told that his life was in danger. The response was similar to that of Glover and Hanlon. Perhaps rather stronger.

The detective went on to add: "We are continually obstructed in our inquiries by the immediate families of the murder victims. People who have lost family have openly warned other members of their family and associates not to speak to the police and that they would deal with the matter themselves. This makes it difficult for us as we obviously need evidence before we can go to court." The conference was also told that there had been a number of very serious assaults in the east end, some of which could have resulted in murder, but for the skills of the medical profession. The victims of these attacks were saying nothing to the police. The detectives also confirmed publicly that the Thompson family had been "most reluctant" to cooperate with them in the hunt for the killer or killers of young Arthur. Assistant Chief Constable Hugh Paton said that these obstructions would not stop the inquiry and he appealed for the public to be of assistance. He added: "I wouldn't say that we had gang warfare but we have criminals involved with the drugs scene and criminals using firearms." From this distance in time the caveat on gang warfare seems more than a trifle semantic. The detectives told the assembled hacks that the drug scene in Glasgow was "a very lucrative business" and this was reflected by the extreme measures employed by those fighting to control it. The police went on to say that there was no evidence that the recent killings were carried out by a London hit team as some had speculated. All the same, they were liaising with the Metropolitan and other UK police forces. As this most remarkable and unusually frank press conference drew to a close Detective Chief Superintendent Pat Connor, the man heading the investigation into the three murders, appealed for witnesses who had seen Glover or Hanlon on the nights before their deaths. He was also looking for sightings of the blue Orion. But that wall of silence, so familiar to the police down the years, was not easily breached. The size of the operation was emphasised with the information that two large teams, one based at Baird Street police station and the other at London Road police station had been set up to investigate the crimes. Officers from the Scottish Crime Squad and the Serious Crime Squad were involved and additional mobile and foot patrols had been drafted into the east end. The police were adamant: "This inquiry will be properly resourced. The pursuit of crime in Strathclyde will not be impeded."

When all this activity was over Paul Ferris appeared in the dock in what would turn out to be the longest running trial in Scottish criminal history. It ran for fifty-four days and cost around three-quarters of a million, by some estimates. Three hundred witnesses were heard. The charge of killing young Arthur while acting with Robert Glover and Joseph Hanlon was only one of seven, if clearly the most important, faced by Ferris. Donald Findlay Q.C. conducted the defence and the judge was Lord McCluskey. The trial provided weeks of entertainment for the newspaper readers who followed the tale as it unfolded in all its complexity.

Hundreds of thousands of words were spoken, all recorded verbatim by a team of around eight court shorthand writers. One *Herald* reporter claimed that he had filled forty large notebooks. Among the productions in this mammoth trial were a bullet proof vest, ammunition cases, several firearms and cartridge cases.

The gangland love of colourful nicknames was a feature with such characters as Brian "Square Go" Graham, William "the Rock" McLeod, "Snazz" Adams, William "Tootsie" Lobban, John "Jonah" McKenzie, William "Gillie" Gillen and David "Soagy" Logue all mentioned. Gangland has long been a fruitful source of odd nicknames and if some of the Glasgow ones are a touch esoteric the Mafia tended to be less obtuse with the likes of "Pittsburgh Phil", "Irish Eyes" Duggan and a long-time Cicero aide of Al Capone who was known as "Batty", which was not a reflection on his mental state – though it might well have been – but rather a tribute to his skill with the baseball bat, no ball involved.

There were some moments of humour to enliven the long days in court and Lord McCluskey even discussed chess, a game in which the nimble-brained accused had an interest and some undoubted skill. As told in *Glasgow's Hard Men*, the case was another notable success for Donald Findlay, who began an address to the jury: "The seasons have come and gone, a general election been won and lost, according to your point of view, and Royal marriages have waxed and waned."

During the trial the credibility of the case against Ferris was consistently destroyed by Findlay and in the end there was a spectacular verdict: not guilty on all charges. So Paul Ferris could stand smiling to his supporters from the courtyard steps and walk away a free man. For the moment. For fate had other plans for the baby-faced young gangster and he was to be caged for other crimes. But that is a tale for later in this book.

An interesting little diversion in this most lengthy of trials was the appearance of Arthur Thompson Snr in the witness box. Asked directly if he was a crime Godfather in Glasgow he stuck to his story that he was simply a business man. He claimed that the allegations that he was a criminal overlord were nonsense and his sense of humour surfaced with a remark that he would have to stuff his mouth with cotton wool and speak like Don Corleone. He claimed that the conviction that sent young Arthur to jail was a police stitch-up. Asked if his son's death could have anything to do with the drugs trade his answer was "nothing at all". When a letter from Dennis Woodman, a witness, was read out referring to him as the Godfather of Glasgow who worked for the Krays, he described the writer as "a nut".

Ferris was free but Bobby Glover and Joe "Bananas" Hanlon were dead. Both had been mentioned, of course, on the Ferris charge sheet as allegedly acting with him in the killing of the "Fat Boy". Both these characters had form. Glover had been given bail shortly before the murder after an incident in which a man was knee-capped. Hanlon was reputed to be an enforcer, and all-round hard man, for the drug runners known as the Barlanark team.

As is normal in murder inquiries the bodies were held for a considerable period of time before being released for burial. But when that happened the were events heavily covered by the media. Indeed around this time scuffles between those mourning loved ones who had died in the drug wars and the media were becoming commonplace and at Old Monklands cemetery in Coatbridge members of the Glover family chased photographers away. Earlier at Old Shettleston Church the minister, the Rev. Robert Tuton, had told the congregation: "Much has been written and said. We don't know exactly what happened nor the motive and I won't concern myself with them today. What we do know is that the events have led to lots of pain, suffering and misery. A wife is without a husband, a little boy without a father, a mother without a son and a family without a brother." Words that depict the reality behind the masses of flowers that colour gangland funerals throughout the world.

The wives and mothers of the footsoldiers in the gang wars receive little attention from the press but Robert Tuton's remarks showed insight into the anguish many of them live with. Bobby Glover's mother gave another example in an interview after a verbal spat with Paul Ferris who had placed an advert in a local paper marking the fifth anniversary of Glover's death. The redoubtable Kathy Glover said: "I knew nothing about my son's life but I knew he was up to no good. I always let him know that I loved him as a son but didn't like what he did."

It is easy to suspect that such sentiments have been felt by hundreds, if not thousands, of Glasgow mothers whose sons chose to run with the sordid excitement of the gangs rather than pursue a lawful life.

10

UNDERCOVER OPERATION

In the annals of criminology there is a history of undercover operations in fact and fiction. No less a person than the legendary Sherlock Holmes uses his talent for disguise, much chronicled by the faithful Dr Watson, to good effect in Conan Doyle's short story "His Last Bow". But it took two years of the life of the Baker Street sleuth to infiltrate the defences of a dastardly German spy in Britain and thwart his evil plans.

In the seventies Glasgow gangland was involved in a remarkable and controversial real-life undercover operation. But it lasted a much shorter period than Holmes' undercover escape, just four months. It came about when a teacher in an approved school was invited by one of his pupils to join a gang on the streets of Maryhill at weekends in order that he could more fully understand the background of boys who ended up in such institutions. It was an invitation fraught with danger but an invitation that provided the chance for a unique social experiment. The undercover investigator was naturally secretive about his identity and when he came to write a book about his experiences (*A Glasgow Gang Observed*) he used the pseudonym of James Patrick. He met and studied one gang twelve times between October 1966 and January 1967, a winter's tale with a difference. His book, which was not published till 1973, ran into the usual flak from the head-in-the-sand brigade, more concerned with some sanitised view of the city than the reality of life on the streets.

By now the author was a lecturer on educational psychology at an English university. He clashed on television, his identity disguised, with the then Lord Provost William Gray and others. On Scottish Television's *Dateline* programme he said he would return to his native city to bring up his family there "yet while there was a marvellous side to Glasgow this could not disguise the delinquency there". He denied that the use of a pseudonym was a ploy to create melodrama and sell the book. He said that since he had ceased to associate with the gang, two boys had been murdered. "That is not melodrama, that is tragedy. I have a family and relatives in Glasgow. I must protect them as much as myself."

He was also attacked, on stronger ground, on the morality of such a book by the assistant chief constable, William Ratcliffe, who said: "It is nonsense that someone on the staff of an approved school should run about with a gang. The leader of the gang, Tim, knew who Mr Patrick was and this was bound to have an effect on the boy." He added that the book had not added one iota of information about the sum total of knowledge about gangs in the city.

The author justified his actions by saying it was difficult for the staff of the school to deal with boys coming from gang culture when the school staff knew next to nothing about them.

It was an entertaining stushie that took up much media attention at the time and highlighted yet again the old tensions about on one hand allegedly sensationalising the gangs and on the other ignoring them. But to my mind the police chief's jibe about this account not adding to knowledge of the gangs and how they operated was well wide of the mark. Perhaps this detailed picture of the life of a street-corner gang at the time was familiar to the men in blue but for many citizens it was an intriguing view into what was almost an alien way of life.

This was a different sort of gang to the groups of the thirties or the organised professional criminal types of the Thompsons and Norvals. This was strictly street-corner stuff. At this time the Maryhill Fleet were a well known group but there were around twenty other gangs of various sizes in the area. Incidentally the members seldom referred to gangs, preferring to use the word "team". And it was the Young Team that Patrick joined for his weekends of adventure and danger. For this he donned his disguise Holmes style . . . "a midnight blue suit, with a twelve-inch middle vent, three inch flaps over the side pockets, and a light blue handkerchief with a white polka dot (to match my tie) in the top pocket". Interestingly fashion can have its own dangers – in the sixties a youth ended up in the Royal Infirmary with eight broken toes, an injury caused by his dedication to wearing Italian winkle picker style shoes. Patrick had allowed his hair to grow long and had cut down his nails, leaving them ragged and dirty.

Right away over pints in a pub he was to witness a mindless attack on a customer who was hit on the head with a lemonade bottle by one of the team and kicked in the stomach when on the floor. Patrick intervened to save the man from further injury by pushing his friend Tim out of the door. Then it was a case of "run like fuck". Frighteningly no one involved seemed to have any rational reason for the attack, it just happened. Patrick had got into this partly because Tim had told him the staff of the approved school didn't appreciate the pressure on the boys when at home for weekends. This was an early demonstration of the problems of trying to stay out of trouble. Tim had asked his teacher to Maryhill to see "whit the score wis" and it had some surprises. Random violence apart, there was much hanging around street corners with not much happening except observations on the passing scene, like the verdict on one girl who passed by – "I've seen mair fat on a cold chip". Or a reference to someone with a dose of the John Knox, i.e. pox.

Scars, Mars Bars in rhyming slang, were worn with pride. Just how deeply ingrained that sort of thinking is can be illustrated by a court tale of a girl who was slashed. The attacker used a razor blade on a girl on three occasions. And in sentencing him the sheriff commented that in a certain class that sort of thing seemed to be a "badge of honour and a style of living". In his defence the accused said that the victim was not averse to using a sharp

138

implement herself and took pride in the mark on her face. Chillingly, the court was told she had said to her assailant, whom she knew, "Use the razor on me and make me a hard woman."

To these young teams it seemed often that territory was everything – to cross into another gang's patch and daub your slogan on a wall was a major triumph.

You suspect that if the experiment was repeated today there would be many similar findings. The major gangs of today like the Barlanark Team and the successors to the Thompsons share an ability to generate newspaper headlines in the fashion of the Redskins, Conks and the Beehives of the past, but operate in different ways, mostly fighting over control of the drugs trade. Teenage street-corner gangs, on the other hand, are less subject to change. The hairstyles and mode of dress may change and fashion can play a role within a gang, but underneath the back to front baseball caps of today there lurks a similar need for collective violence and marking out of territory as in the past. And a thirst for excitement. Patrick's book which, apart form the more lurid episodes, contained much valuable research into gangs, was the result of years of study. A more immediate picture of gang life was obtained by a *Herald* reporter in the sixties. There was no undercover stuff here, no double life as a gang member one minute, a social worker the next. He simply got hold of a youngster who could talk and produced an article with the heading: "The Thrill of Danger in Joining a Glasgow Gang".

His informant was Tommy, a seventeen-year-old "typical" Glaswegian who lived in a tenement, had a passion for football, went to the dancing every weekend, and was said to be fashion-conscious. Tommy was a member of the Tongs and along with his mates was only too ready to talk about what that meant. The unnamed reporter said that Tommy was well aware of court procedure as a result of appearances on charges of loitering or fighting with members of rival gangs and his convictions made him something of a hero to his pals.

He gave lengthy and vivid accounts of fights and talked with obvious pride of his ability with a "chib" (weapon) and the times he had "claimed" (attacked) another youth. He even boasted of having been a victim of an attack. It was said that in this respect he was no different from other gang members: "The thrill to be experienced from a constant fear for one's own safety is an integral part of gang life." Tommy provided an insight into the language of the gangs. A "seconder" was anyone with a scar on his face, so-called because he had come off second best. A "hander" is anyone who will come to your aid in a fight, and to be "huckled" is to be arrested.

Though not the most impressive piece of research into gang culture, this in-your-face form of interviewing produced some good answers. In an effort to find a motive for gang violence Tommy was asked why he disliked members of other gangs. "Because they hate us" was the dispiriting reply. At this point he mentioned one of his friends had been attacked by the Fleet and plans to get even were afoot.

The belief that it is all about territory was briefly questioned as Tommy mentioned that many groups, or gangs, tended to frequent the same cafés or dance halls. But districts are associated with individual gangs. This report placed the Fleet in Maryhill, the Cumbie in the Gorbals, Buck in Drumchapel, Shamrock in Townhead. The Toi and Toon concentrated their efforts in the city centre.

The situation is confused because as other observers have noted, the names of major gangs are often adopted by smaller groups in other areas. Tommy was adamant for example that the real Tongs only existed in Calton despite many other gangs calling themselves Tongs this or Tongs that.

The subject of leadership was discussed with some surprising results. The belief that everyone wants to be top dog was questioned. One youngster put it: "The worst thing is to get a reputation as a 'big man'. Everyone is then trying to prove he is better." But others in this group seemed to wallow in the glory of being head of the team and worked hard to climb to the top. At the height of the motor scooter craze a highly personalised set of wheels was a must, one gang leader even had his whole machine chromed. There were other attempts to create a mystique and "bonding". One highly organised gang was said to insist that its members wore bright red socks all the time to enable them to be recognised as a friend in a gang fight. This was the sort of thinking that also prevailed in the heyday of the football "casuals" who followed teams to matches wearing matching woollen sweaters and created mayhem fighting opposition supporters or simply fighting in streets or bars near stadiums.

Tommy claimed that there was no problem with recruitment. As older members dropped out, perhaps heading for respectability, or more likely a life of more sophisticated crime, youngsters were queuing up to join.

Tommy also highlighted the continuing practice of "junior" sections. In the thirties the Billy Boys had the KKK as a youth offshoot. Tommy was proud that his brother was a member of the Young Tongs.

A Glasgow Gang Observed makes much of a penchant for carrying weapons that seems to have been little diluted down the years. Operation Blade launched by the police as recently as 1993 turned up some remarkable figures. The then chief constable, Leslie Sharp, initiated a stop and search blitz by the police and a month-long amnesty for handing in weapons called "Bin the Knife – Save a Life". The results were a tad more spectacular than in the Easterhouse amnesty dealt with earlier in this book. Forty-two people were arrested after the searches, charged with being in possession of offensive weapons, a haul which included a Samurai sword and a machete. The use of swords as a gang weapon dates back to the First World War and before and you wonder where on earth they all come from. The possibility of secret sword smugglers in the twenty-first century is too bizarre to contemplate!

The razor blade is less exotic but perhaps more dangerous. And they were carried by children as young as nine. One mother was astonished to find that her nine-year-old carried a blade and ended up in juvenile court in Govan accused of slashing the coat of a girl aged ten. Relatives of the boy said all the other boys had blades and that they were members of a miniature gang. This case was continued for three months on the understanding that the accused's mother paid for repairs to the coat.

Earlier than Patrick's infiltration of the gangs and the observations of Tommy there had been, back in the early fifties, one of the periodic outbreaks of calls for the use of corporal punishment to control these sorts of corner-boy gangs. The enthusiasm for birching and whipping was quite remarkable. "Bring Back the Lash" was a staple newspaper headline. In one case Sir Victor Warren, when Lord Provost, was approached by the parents of a thirteen-year-old who had been attacked by a gang on the banks of the Forth and Clyde canal. After this meeting he told the press "I am more convinced than ever that the Acts which govern the magistrates in dealing with juvenile crime are inadequate. If hooliganism is going to be put down there is only one way – the use of the strap or cane.

"Today the only children who are allowed to be whipped are the children of aristocrats at Eton and Harrow. The sooner this old-fashioned policy is adopted for the masses the sooner we shall have proper conduct in this city."

Such cries for cane, strap and birch came at a time when Restricted Diet No.1 – bread and water – was still in use in Borstals "when other forms of punishment have failed". Just a year after this outburst by the Lord Provost, who seemed only a smidgeon less harsh than the chief of police mentioned in a previous chapter who wanted to beat young criminals till they bled, the Government published a fascinating report on boys from approved schools. Much of the research was done in English establishments but there is no reason to suppose the findings did not apply to Scotland as well. These kids were inveterate cinema-goers visiting, "the pictures" up to ten times a week. The report said that "the fact that delinquents go to the cinema frequently is, obviously, no indication that going to the cinema necessarily causes delinquency. There is, however, a tendency nowadays to rely overmuch on mechanical entertainment which has reached such a pitch of intensity and power that it makes people punch drunk. When boys have learned to withstand the excitements of screen and radio, the sensational press, the even more sensational 'comic', the blare and glare of the pin table saloon, and the noise of jazz bands, they are not easily influenced by a mere schoolmaster." James Patrick, one suspects, would be in agreement here. Discussing the average intelligence of the approved school boy, their vocabulary was found to be limited, if expressive, and not what was called in these days standard English. The meagreness of their cultural background was "incredible". At the time of a General Election only two boys out of hundreds knew the name of even the main political parties. When George Bernard Shaw died no boy had even heard of him. Even what was going on in the world of football was a mystery to most. Taking a walk with such a boy was interesting said the report. The countryside meant nothing to them but a passing car or a scrap dump was immediately spotted as having potential for delinquency. Every opportunity for crime – like trees overhanging a garden – was noted, almost subconsciously. If nothing else they had an expert eye for the main chance. A similarity with the Young Team.

The sort of neighbourhood gang infiltrated by James Patrick has, down the years, been mirrored in many areas of Glasgow. There have even been all-girl gangs with a similar structure. Back in the 1940s young girls, no doubt aping the thuggery of their boyfriends, formed gangs like the She Tongs and Young She Cumbie. But recently the police have stated that female gang membership only extended to a few hangers-on and an outfit known as the Queen Street Posse whose object seemed to be shoplifting sprees in the city centre.

But female violence was by no means unheard of in the nineties. Liz Ingram, who made a documentary for Channel 4 called *Possil Girls – We Are Here*, found plenty of young girls ready to wade into a street fight. She found some who could fight violently with their

143

friends one day and forget it the next. But quantifying the number of girl gang members has, even since the days of the Queen of the Nudies, been difficult since statistics often don't give the sex of the offender.

Interestingly Patrick, who had suffered so much criticism for his dual role as social worker and pretend gang member, was attacked from a different quarter almost as soon as his work was published. Another commentator, Ian Mathie, a probation officer, claimed that many of his observations had become out of date in the period between investigation and publication.

In a report on mini-muggings in schools he wrote that we had moved into the age of the teeny-bopper. "These kids are in the 12 to 14 age group, have long hair and are at the pre-pubertal stage. Nevertheless they frequently carry weapons and drink cheap wine. There has recently been an escalation of their activities, which are no longer centred on the youth and employment exchanges, but on schools." The children involved were said to show complete contempt for "all manifestations of the establishment" including school, police, the children's hearings and the social work department. As ever in Glasgow this produced counter argument, on this occasion from councillor Dan Docherty who suggested that the stories of twelve-year-olds slugging cheap wine were wildly exaggerated, as were the tales of mini-muggings.

But there can be no doubt that there was some truth in it and that the culprits were potential recruits ready to graduate to the gangs.

The same year, Glasgow was getting what an old hack would call "bad ink" in America, potentially a potent source of income for our tourist industry. Glasgow was one of the five most dangerous cities in Europe according to no less a journal than *Time* magazine. We were according to the American scribes up there in the bad boy stakes with London, Frankfurt, West Berlin and Rome.

This was colourful stuff. The magazine warned that when a gang member approaches a fight with a stiff limp it is not necessarily an indication of an old injury – beware "in his pants leg is a full-length ceremonial sword". Glasgow was said to have a faster rising crime rate than any other major city in Britain. "The local speciality is the rampant assault – mostly bar room brawling and vicious rioting among members of teenage gangs."

The report on crime in Europe had been provoked by criticism of the safety of the streets of New York and it is to *Time*'s credit that the magazine had to admit that none of the European cities it criticised was as dangerous as the Empire State city itself.

And in the ensuing controversy the redoubtable Evelyn Schaffer, a psychologist just back from a visit to the States, could say that to call Glasgow a little Chicago was a gross exaggeration – in 1972 Glasgow had twelve murders whereas Chicago had 968 and New York 1650.

However any student of gangland Glasgow will note that the item on the sword is not all that far-fetched and in 1973 the city was providing real and bloody evidence that the teenage gangs were a major problem to the city, if not to tourists.

The outbreaks of battling seem to occur almost at random in various districts. Sometimes, for a spell, much of the aggro is in one area, a few years later it is in another. When the *Time* article was written there was particular unrest in Pollok, Priesthill and Kinning Park. The chief constable at the time was perhaps Glasgow's most famous, after Sillitoe, David McNee who went on to lead the Met in London and get involved in all sorts of controversy there. Sir David, as he now is, had many similarities to his famous predecessor. Sillitoe was known to his men as the Captain and McNee's nickname was the Hammer of the Neds, some indication of his success and renown in an area where a copper has to win respect the hard way. McNee was more of an interventionist than Sillitoe, a man of deep religious conviction who felt good policing could help regenerate areas and improve social conditions for the inhabitants. Like Sillitoe he used the best of modern technology, mobile support units and saturation policing in problem areas, and the like. He also foresaw the benefit of helicopters though Glasgow's purse strings were too tight to indulge him in this area. He had many successes, especially a war against illegal money lenders who cause so much misery to West of Scotland families.

When he left in 1977 for the onerous task of running the Met, a new splurge of gang violence was blighting the east end. The gangs involved were the Torch and the Spur. This was a battle to be fought not with knives (which had largely taken over from razors at this point) but with guns. Two Barrowfield youngsters were arrested on charges of having guns and ammunitions with intent to endanger life. This was a warning call to detectives who saw the looming power struggle and went public to say: "We don't know where they are getting the guns from but it is vital we get hold of the weapons before someone is killed."

The two would-be teenage gunmen were found guilty and when led from court one of them turned and shouted to detectives: "You had better not be here when I get out." Outside the court in the corridors jeering associates of the accused were involved in a scuffle with the police. The court had heard a dramatic tale that illustrated just how bad the problem was – armed detectives had swooped on a derelict tenement on the outskirts of the infamous Barrowfield scheme, of which more is to be said later, and found one of the youths carrying a gun, broken down into three pieces, and the other the cartridges. A detective told them he was armed and they were to walk slowly out of the hallway. One of the youths told the detectives "we are getting hammered by the Spur. You know what they did to my brother." In court the jury were shown the gun which had a swastika on the butt and the words "Torch kill for fun" and "To Spur from Torch – Boom ya Bass" on the barrel. After the trial a police spokesman said the tragedy was that the gangs were finding it easier to get hold of arms. The investigation had started after a gun was fired in a taxi in the Barrowfield area and spent cartridges were found lying in the street after rival gang battles. This particular gun was of Russian manufacture and the police didn't have a clue how it had ended up in a Glasgow scheme.

This horrific incident in the early seventies had helped catapult the scheme into the consciousness of the Glasgow newspaper reader. It was not a place much visited by the douce burghers of the city other than in voyeuristic forays into the tabloids.

It lay in the shadow of Celtic Park, the east end's Field of Dreams, where the roar of the crowd echoed into the black sky on European football nights when the mightiest teams of Europe took on Celtic. And often they went home with respect for the brand of football played by the Scots, men who had come up the hard way through junior football or lesser leagues and had none of the glamour associated with the stars of Inter Milan, Barcelona, Roma and the like but who in 1967 had made history as the first British team to win the European cup, something all these years later that seems to be have disappeared from the collective memory of the patronising English TV pundits of the Beckham era. The stadium which had so many great nights of success and so dominated the area physically was ironically nicknamed Paradise, a nod in the direction of a graveyard in the area. But Barrowfield was as far removed from an earthly paradise as you could imagine. The nickname of the old corrugated iron-covered terracing at Celtic's stadium, the Jungle, was more apt.

The newspaper feature-writers of the time made many an expedition into this earthy urban jungle. Sometimes on the lookout for good news, that can be hard to find, they unearthed good citizens who were struggling to earn a crust and bring up a decent family in surroundings of great deprivation. Violence of the mean and bloody kind was an everyday hazard for such decent folk thrown by fate, and a housing shortage, into such a bear pit. Much of the crime in the area went unreported because of the fear, the sickening fear of inevitable retribution, that gripped honest toilers who had to witness the criminality of their neighbours. Revenge for telling tales to the cops could be swift and drastic. Being a reporter going to the scheme meant talking to folk who just would not give their name, even if they were brave enough to talk to you themselves. "We don't want to be identified. We can't be. We're afraid what they might do to us or the kids." It was a frequent plea.

The council was, of course, aware of the problem and threw money at it without much success. A two million pound modernisation scheme might have improved the quality of the housing but it didn't create a safe haven. This was a familiar Glasgow scenario. Some years later in Bankend Street – to become familiar to every citizen after the horrors of the ice cream wars – at one stage £11,000 was spent on every house providing new roofs, neat balconies and other appealing external features. A few years later the politicians had to acknowledge reality and bulldoze the lot.

Back in Barrowfield in the seventies one family put the problems of the area into perspective: "It used to be a scheme where you could walk in safety. But now you take a chance every time to walk down the road. We used to go out every Saturday night, now you are scared to cross the doorstep. There are two gangs in one street, the Torch and the Spur, and when they are on the prowl life's just not worth living."

So bad was the scheme's reputation at that time that some firms refused to make deliveries and it is said a washing machine was once delivered with a police escort. Many families said they would stay in the area if violence could be eradicated. But even those who wanted to leave for leafier new towns or suburbs found difficulties. A Barrowfield address on an application form often meant refusal. It was no help to have been a long time resident, there was no respect for even that. One family who lived in the area for years returned from holiday to find every window in the house broken and said: "They don't care who they do it to. You could know them for years and they would still do it to you. It's bedlam sometimes. What can you do?" A cry of despair that could be repeated a thousand fold.

There were occasional outbreaks of comparative peace for the inhabitants of this benighted place – the times when the majority of the villains were under lock and key in Barlinnie just down the road. No wonder there was strong support for the throw-away-the-key theory of justice in Barrowfield.

The Bench, if not in total agreement, recognised the problem and Lord Wheatley, the Lord Justice-Clerk, warned in 1975 that members of the gangs would find their sentences on the increase. Rejecting an appeal against conviction by an eighteen-year-old who had used a knife in an assault, he said: "This curse which is afflicting the country at present and is particularly acute in Glasgow has got to be wiped out. At one stage in the history of Glasgow razor slashing was common. To a great extent the use of the razor has been eliminated, unfortunately to be replaced with an equally deadly weapon, the knife. But if there is any danger of razor slashing rearing its head again in Glasgow the sooner it is stamped out the better."

Maybe appealing the six-year sentence wasn't a good idea. Lord Wheatley went on to say that "his only worry was whether or not the sentence was long enough. I can tell you that if I had been the presiding judge it would have been greater." The court had been told that one of the victims of the assault had received no fewer than forty-nine stitches to his head and was permanently disfigured. The law lord rounded off his advice to the knifemen and potential slashers thus: "I want to sound this further note of warning on increased sentencing. There are gangs roaming the streets with offensive weapons and prepared to use them at the drop of a hat. If offences continue, sentences will be stepped up further."

There were occasional blinks of hope in this seventies gang gloom. One remarkable Cranhill woman broke the unwritten code of not getting involved. This was long before "have a go" interventions had become so common that the police took to warning against them. A forty-nine-year-old woman, Joan Nicolletti, heard shouts outside her window at 11 p.m. and looked out. A young man was surrounded by a gang who had knocked him down. Subsequently it turned out he had been walking with his girlfriend when out of the blue he was hit over the head with a bottle. Mrs Nicolletti ran from her home shouting "leave him alone you scum". All but one of these "brave" gangland warriors ran for their life. And the one who remained regretted it for Mrs Nicolletti, who had taken the injured man into her house, kept her nerve and identified him at an identity parade. Sadly an all too rare tale.

By the mid-seventies Barrowfield was clearly identified as a problem area and ideas emerged to try to do something about it. An eight-day community festival run by social workers was held. Celebrities rallied round in true Glasgow fashion. The famous names of Glasgow have never shied away from lending a hand in areas of deprivation and crime, and Celtic's legendary manager Jock Stein took time off from training his squad, writer Cliff Hanley, famous for among other books *Dancing in the Streets*, took time away from the typewriter, and Tiger Tim Stevens, a radio Clyde disc jockey with an eccentric attitude and a huge listening following also took time to help out. Activities included a yard of ale drinking competition – something of horses for courses here! – a football film show, a celebrity football match, a talent competition, a street play involving local children and a parade through the scheme. It may not have won the war against the thugs but it was an enjoyable spark of hope.

Another came in 1978 when the "silent majority" in the gang-ridden area were praised in the papers for standing up for themselves. A court report said that: "For years families in Barrowfield have kept a frightened silence about the vicious thugs on their doorstep. A wild night of terror did something to change that, at least on this occasion. The police were called to the scheme when cars were wrecked, house windows and doors smashed and members of the Spur ended in dock." Sheriff Norman McLeod pulled no punches: "This type of uncivilised savagery is the sort of misfortune that the decent folk of Barrowfield have had to suffer for too long and too often." The sheriff praised locals for speaking out, and called it a dreadful case. Both youths before him admitted being "part of a riotous mob which conducted itself in violent and tumultuous manner to the great terror and alarm of

the lieges and that they brandished swords and other weapons."
Such was life in a Glasgow scheme in the mid-seventies. Weapons
brandished apart from the swords included pickaxe handles and
sickles. Among the cars smashed up was an invalid carriage. The
mob when not wrecking cars went along streets hammering on
doors with their weapons as the householders cowered in fear
behind the flimsy protection of an inch or so of wood.

But several phoned the police and were courageous enough to
identify the members of this terrifying mob.

Some of the weapons were found to have Spur 78 engraved on
them and the two arrested replied "Spur rule" when charged and
"I'll do it right the next time".

It is scary when reading such accounts to realise how strong the
don't-mention-what-is-going-on lobby was in those days. How
they managed to evade the evidence of the mayhem all around
them and convince themselves that somehow or other if only they
kept quiet about what was going on it would go away, is mind-
boggling. But tell that to a frightened family hiding behind a
flimsy door while wild drunken thugs, waving weapons, try to
hammer it down.

The two teenage thugs involved in this instance were given five
years each in a young offenders' institution and Lord Wheatley in
handing down the sentences noted that although the wrecking
took place in Barrowfield there were other places in the city where
similar mobs roamed the street. He also observed that this sort of
thing also happened in other apparently civilised cities in the
world.

The leader writers in both the tabloids and broadsheets had no
answer to the problem other than to believe that until some better
way was found to solve it, heavy sentences were a must. Decent
folk, themselves sentenced to life in deprived streets, at least
deserved safety.

A problem for the police was how easily thugs could be
provoked. Not long after the horrific riot described above, another
outrage took place. The reason? Scotland's defeat by Peru in the

football World Cup in far off Argentina. You might have expected that even the most hardened young member of a gang team would find it no surprise to hear of a defeat for his country at the hands of football minnows. It has happened often enough. But no, a gang who had watched another unexpected defeat and humiliation relayed from South America to home TV screens responded by running from their homes enraged by the display. Police called to Stamford Street in the scheme found mobs of armed youths chanting gang slogans and challenging each other to a fight. The defence lawyer for one of the accused opined in court that the offence was "one of many which arose out of the now infamous and humiliating Scotland football defeat by Peru". So much for it's only a game.

Barrowfield wasn't the only area to suffer. Similar carnage was taking place in Haghill between the Goucho and the Powrie gangs. Police were so concerned that they had set up a special anti-terror squad for the area, but the old bogey of victims being afraid to talk was hindering the operation. But one night in a midnight battle the Gaucho and the Powrie went too far. They marched twenty abreast through Haghill shouting gang slogans and waving swords. A girl and a youth were shot in the ensuing battle but this time eyewitnesses were prepared to talk and the jury heard lurid tales of the violence. One defence lawyer remarked, not without humour and accuracy, that the case was "perhaps more appropriate to the west of Texas than the west of Scotland". A detective told of taking an anonymous phone call in which the caller told him: "You had better go armed. He's got a shooter and will shoot the first polis he sees." When the police got to the scene the gunman crashed through a window in true Hollywood style and ran to hide in a graveyard where the detective, gun in hand, cornered him against a wall. Wild west stuff in the east end.

The life of a lawman in these parts was difficult and dangerous. Even after an arrest was made, no one was safe. Back in Barrowfield the Spur were at it again and two policemen were attacked and pinned down by a hail of stones, bricks, bottles, and sticks thrown by a mob of youths attempting to rescue a man in police custody. It was a grotesque scene: one gang member was heard shouting "I am mental. Us Spurs are going to kill you police. Come on boys let's get tooled up." While the two unfortunate officers radioed for assistance they were showered with missiles. There were shouts of "Kill the pigs" and "get Mick free". The officers at the end of this sickening violence were saved from severe injury by the arrival of reinforcements. Such episodes, which happened in the twenties and thirties and during the First World War as well, are illustrations of the provocation that faced the street policeman. Lawyers, journalists, policemen and witnesses were running out of adjectives to describe such events. Colourful language was part of almost every court case.

Even George Square, overlooked by the magnificence of the City Chambers, the Head Post Office and the elegant North British Hotel, and peppered with statues of the good and the great of history, wasn't safe from the violence. Here the late-night buses gathered to take revellers home from the dance halls and pubs to the quiet of the suburbs. On a normal night there was trouble enough from the drunks and panhandlers who gathered in the wee small hours to pester the bus crews and their respectable passengers. But one January night the Square excelled itself and after a night of gang warfare it was described in court as "looking like Armageddon".

Ambulances ferried the injured to hospital, passengers fled from a besieged bus and a frightened taxi driver had to drive through the mob to reach safety. The judge in the ensuing court case Lord Maxwell said he was surprised taxi drivers were willing to operate in the city itself. "They must be remarkably brave men," he said. The prosecution had told of large crowds gathering for the late-night buses when the battle started. One gang invaded a bus, stabbing a youth and punching and kicking another. A third fled across the square pursued by a large gang screaming gang slogans and throwing missiles. After he was felled by a bottle he got up and managed to jump into a taxi stopped at traffic lights. Moments later the cabbie found himself marooned in his car by the mob. Prosecuting counsel said: "He became extremely apprehensive for though he has seen various affrays late at night in various parts of the city he had never seen anything like this. He reversed his taxi into the mob and managed to escape and attract police attention."

As if all this wasn't bad enough, as the decade ended there were signs that really young offenders were getting more sophisticated in their approach to crime. Two young boys were caught after a £10,000 Gorbals wage snatch, and a couple of fifteen-year-old girls were charged with thieving from pensioners under the guise of selling raffle tickets for good causes.

And some of James Patrick's observations on the role played by girlfriends were underlined in a murder trial. Girls aged sixteen to eighteen told the court how they had helped the murdering gang by hiding the machete used in the brutal killing, cleaning the bloodstained clothes of the boys who had launched the attack, lending a jacket to a boy who had left his own, stained with blood, in a café, and hidden a weapon under a bed on the murder night.

The evidence was heard in what became known as the Clarkston Murder trial after a young dental student had been killed by a gang in an unprovoked attack involving a boning knife, a knife and a machete. The murder trial made headline news, particularly since it took place in an area not normally thought to be the haunt of gangs, or to hold any particular danger to a youngster on a harmless night out.

Apart from the involvement of this unpleasant assortment of molls, a curious aspect of this case was that thugs from the Castlemilk housing scheme where there was a "team" called Young Cumbie and a team from the more prosperous nearby area of Busby (the members were said to have come from good family backgrounds) had formed a strange alliance to go hunting trouble together. A most unusual happening for the "street-corner" type of gang. Proof that even in gangland there is an exception to every rule – this particular wickedness was not promoted by a territorial dispute.

11

MOTORWAY MADNESS

The eighties were the years when despite all the mayhem that went on in the distant schemes, and occasional outbreaks of violence in the city centre, the balance of opinion was that Glasgow was moving in the right direction as a pleasant place to live.

An architectural revolution changed the face of the city, Mr Happy was busy with his message that Glasgow was Miles Better, the Garden Festival had been a great success, tourists were beating a path to the Burrell Collection, and at the end of this decade of change came the accolade European City of Culture. Even Mrs Thatcher, reviled by the populace with a passion unequalled anywhere in Britain, was saying it was a government success. The Dear Green Place was, as the *Herald* leader writer put it, "somewhat in fashion".

But fashion is often a facade and all the good news about Glasgow in the late eighties and the start of the nineties was not the complete story. Gang violence had made a comeback, albeit in somewhat different guises than before. And in one year there was a leap of 27 per cent in firearms crime in Scotland.

When in difficulties commentators and feature writers tend to reach for the Wild West analogy and so it happened again. Areas were said to be like Fort Apache, the Bronx (actually the wild east if you want to be pedantic) and the wilder parts of Texas. Scotland's eight chief constables called a crisis meeting. This time a more sanguine approach was taken than in previous cyclical crime waves. Rising urban crime was a worldwide problem and the growth of

155

an underclass, and drugs misuse, were all highlighted.

This new era of crime introduced behaviour unheard of in the past. Council workers threatened to boycott work in the Linthaugh Road and Calfhill Road areas of Pollok after a number of attacks. Firemen tackling blazes were even ambushed by gangs of youngsters. Council employees were injured or threatened. And in an astonishing demonstration of biting the hand that feeds you, thousands of pounds worth of damage was done to employees' cars parked at the Lyoncross local repair centre. A fire officer was quoted as saying that "In the run up to Guy Fawkes it was murder in there. It has been happening regularly. It used to be that fire-fighters could go into the roughest areas freely because they were helping the community – now it seems we are fair game." This was a view echoed by firemen in Parkhead, another area where the yobs were in action. Attacks on firemen are no rare occurrence; Strathclyde Brigade logs them and in 2001 there were 157 incidents recorded, but this could only be the tip of a large iceberg since many incidents went unrecorded. And it is not just bricks and verbal abuse that firemen face. Airguns, too, are used in attacks on them. A fireman was even hit in the face with a brick as he gave mouth to mouth resuscitation to an injured man on Glasgow Green. In Haghill an officer wearing breathing apparatus and in the act of fighting a blaze was hit with a brick.

In this new world far removed from the murky closes and stinking backcourts of the thirties, but in some ways equally violent, that familiar figure of city life, the taxi driver found himself in the front line, a target for thugs. "No go" areas for the black hacks and the private hires that lubricate travel in a city where public transport can leave a lot to be desired, were identified. With the extensive tramcar and trolley bus network destroyed, and the subway system a hark back to Victoriana, getting around by bus is time-consuming if not impossible in some cases. The "Joe Baksi" (rhyming slang evolved from the name of the famous American boxer), as the taxi is known, is a significant part of daily life. Pensioners take them to the shops or to visit a friend in the city's hospitals which are particularly hard to get to by public transport. Young mums use them on city shopping expeditions where the return journey, weighed down by well-filled plastic bags, makes the rush hour bus a nightmare. Working men take a Joe Baksi to the pub or bookies. Youngsters use them to head to the leisure centre, weighted down in this case with sports bags. Heavy duty taxi use is a way of life. But in modern day Glasgow there are limits – one of the city's biggest companies produced a list of "no go" areas. Cabs were being attacked by missile-throwing vandals in some streets and the Taxi Owners Association feared that serious injury or accident was a possibility. Drivers tell of gangs of thugs, some as young as ten, lying in wait to ambush them. I experienced this unpleasant phenomenon myself travelling into town recently on a quiet summer Sunday night, in the unexpected confines of Clarkston Road on the southside, when a balloon filled with water, a surprisingly solid object, smashed into the cabby's windscreen causing him to swerve and narrowly miss a lamppost. It was no new experience for this driver and most Glasgow cabbies have plenty of tales of running a barrage of stones and bottles aimed at the cabs by gangs of youths. Makeshift road blocks are on occasion set up by thugs in a bid to make drivers slow down or stop before being attacked.

A favourite ploy is to attack in areas where blocked off roads make escape easy for the attackers. According to the TOA drivers have alternative routes to enable them to pass the danger zones which were listed as: Edgefauld Road and Carlisle Street, Gourlay Street in Springburn, Royston Road, Townhead, Mayfield Street, Ruchill, Panmure Street, Possilpark, Springfield Road, Parkhead, and the Tollcross Park area. But, as I found to my cost, taxi attacks can happen almost anywhere, even in the most respectable of neighbourhoods.

While the gangs battled and vandals went on the rampage in Pollok there was unwanted action north of the river as well. Poor old Easterhouse was still in the front line with rival gangs battling with petrol bombs, swords and axes. This territorial squabbling by gangs around the M8 interchange at Craighall brought one particular incident that made the front pages and shocked the whole city. A thirteen-year-old girl died fleeing across the motorway from battling gangs, from Roystonhill and Germiston.

It is dispiriting to read that despite all the effort poured into Easterhouse over decades by police, social workers and decent folk in the area, in 1993 the chairman of the community council could tell of gangs still battling it out with the old weapons of swords and axes. Of children frightened to walk the streets in case they were attacked by a gang. A tenants' association official said it was really bad after 8 p.m. and that people were scared to go to the bank or post office. History repeated itself once again when the police made vain appeals for people to pass on the names of the villains – in confidence, of course.

The main culprits were the Shamrock from Germiston and the Monks from Dennistoun, but there was said to be a gang war zone stretching from Sighthill and Roystonhill through Blackhill to Easterhouse, all on the north side of the M8. Gangs on the other side of the motorway came from Riddrie through Cranhill to Barlanark. In a sinister development the police said that these outbreaks were not random battles but pre-arranged.

The national media once again latched on to what was happening but the reaction of the city's politicos was more rational in the past. The then Lord Provost Bob Innes said that Glasgow's city of culture status was here to stay and council leader Jean McFadden made the not particularly insightful observation that Glasgow was not the only city suffering from mounting crime, as if that made being mugged any more acceptable. But it was also acknowledged that it was certainly worrying that there was more crime in Glasgow than seems to get reported. And drugs were admittedly a problem to a much greater extent than in the past. But reporting on crime in the city had to be fair and balanced and take in the other more positive aspects of the city. Not an unreasonable plea. In a more sophisticated world than in the past, tourist chiefs saw no let-up in demand.

And it is true that in the nineties and after the turn of the century the city is a major tourist draw and that holidaymakers who will risk Miami and Marseilles are well able to make their own judgements and do not need to be mollycoddled, or indeed deceived, by the crime deniers. Indeed all the old clamour about outside media, TV stations and national newspapers based in London, reporting the bad news to folk who would never know about it otherwise is now redundant thanks to technology. A tourist in Des Moines or Dubai researching a trip to Glasgow has, thanks to the internet, easy access to the latest state of play in the crime culture. All Glasgow's newspapers – which chart the goings-on of the street gangs and the big boys' drugs wars – are on the web and can be read for free on a daily basis. Library databases giving both the history of crime in the city and the current events are available at the drop of a modem. Secrecy or pretending there isn't a problem is no longer an option.

The sort of street violence blighting areas formerly regarded as quiet backwaters, so prominent from the early nineties to this day, should not be confused with the violence of the gangs of the Godfathers. The successors to Norval and Thompson are evil men who ruin lives but who tend to fight among themselves in a different class of war. Off the record police quotes show that the men in blue are only too well aware that the man in the street is unlikely to be caught up in the major league battles. On the other hand, the mini gangs can make life miserable for thousands of people afraid to go about their business in the streets they call home.

An example of this came as recently as spring 2002. In the east end the big boys in the flak jackets and 4x4s were having one of their periodic battles over turf. Miles away on the other side of the river a douce suburb, once thought to be a pleasant place to live in, was experiencing a nightmare. Cardonald is an area where many tenants still tend neat gardens and apply their do-it-yourself skills to Victorian villas. Not so long ago it was a quiet place with a splendid community spirit. Nowadays some of the folk there are of a night trapped behind the privet hedge and their closed blinds, intimidated and afraid. Once the only activity at night was children playing in the streets, now it is a battleground for gangs wielding baseball bats and knives, not to mention machetes. The gangs who come to fight in this area have members as young as twelve and are said to come from Penilee, Craigton (the Gaucho, a name borrowed from the east end) and Pollok, as well as Cardonald. And they use the internet to arrange and publicise their activities. Gangs with their own web pages are cauld kale now. E-mails and expensive mobile phones are used to organise and coordinate trouble. Indeed the police and teachers are anxious to prevent pupils from logging on to such web pages where gangsters are showing off their weapons and drinking on camera. Some folk in the area are even said to be afraid to call 999 in case of retaliation, though there is one tale of a bold granny grabbing a blood-stained baseball bat from fighting youngsters and handing it in to the police. One battleground was Paisley Road West. Local councillor Alastair Watson told a public meeting that "We are talking about a mile-long stretch of road that is being used as a battleground by groups of gangs – it's like the OK Corral." And he was not talking about late night events: sometimes the weapons and the gangs were out on Saturday afternoons when the road was busy with shoppers. Another crisis meeting was told by Marion Pagani, Chairwoman of the Children's Panel, that a police crackdown was not the only solution to teenage gang violence but admitted that the children's panel system had only limited resources. There are only ninety-six secure places in Scotland but children don't always benefit from being locked up.

Not much consolation to a pensioner who told the press that she used to live in New York and was never scared to walk the streets. "But I can tell you I am scared to walk the streets of Cardonald." Not long after MSP Tommy Sheridan moved to the area he chased a gang of thirty youths he found vandalising cars. He wanted more of a police presence on these dangerous streets. Other residents called for a curfew after 9 p.m. but the police pointed out that an experimental curfew in Hamilton had not been extended to other areas. More CCTV cameras were however to be introduced.

Glasgow needs no lessons from other violent areas in the world on gangs, our home grown villains match the evil to be found anywhere. The tabloids are on occasion filled with tales of mobsters using spoons to gouge out eyes and tortures of the sort to make a decent human being feel sick and ashamed of what can go on in a city. A certain introversion and overwhelming involvement in our own gang warfare may have played a role in the city avoiding the minefield of being drawn into the modern sectarian warfare that is taking place a short plane ride across the Irish sea in Ulster. Events in Ireland had some role to play in the days of the Billy Boys who made that well-documented foray to Belfast, pre-war. But, with a few exceptions, both sides of the religious divide managed not to import Northern Ireland's particular brand of mayhem. A cynic might remark with some justification that we have enough action of our own to be going on with. Likewise, after the war, Glasgow seemed for a time to dodge much of the trouble caused by the Chinese triad gangs which were said to have spread around the globe and which had infiltrated Oriental communities in London, Manchester, Birmingham and Bristol. But there were spectacular exceptions with horrific incidents in the late eighties and early nineties.

Detectives from the Royal Hong Kong police were called in to help with the case of Cheng Pik-yai, almost hacked to death in his Renfield Street restaurant. Mr Cheng got involved in a financial dispute that sparked the attack with meat cleavers and machetes, the "myriad of swords" punishment of a secret society. He used his martial skill in a desperate fight for his life. His knees were battered with metal bars and he was hacked into the bone by knives.

What were said to be reliable sources in the then colony were reported as believing one of the dreaded Chinese underground secret societies and "hired knives" up from England were involved. The Hong Kong police force, which at one time used the services of legendary Glasgow newspaper man Drew Rennie to look after its image, was busy indeed. Its Organised Crime Bureau – world experts in the spread of the triads – was at the time of the Glasgow investigation also cooperating with police forces in America, Australia, and Europe as well as the Far East. It was feared that elements of the three largest societies, the Wo Sing Wo, the Wo On Lok and the dreaded 14k had reached Scotland. Previous to the attack on Cheng Pik-yai, another restaurant owner, Philip Wong, had been chopped to pieces.

In the world of the triads to break the vows of a secret society, to refuse to pay extortion money, or to talk to the police was extremely dangerous. Out of the dark men with hatchets would appear without warning.

Glasgow police tend not to ignore a problem and an international conference was called to allow officers to pool their knowledge. This and other initiatives like community policing helped take some of the steam out of what, given the size of the Chinese population in Glasgow, could have turned into a major problem.

12

"A BLOODY MURDEROUS ACT"

In the recent history of crime and gangs in Glasgow one incident stands above all in the public memory – the ice cream wars murders. The full horror of what happened in Bankend Street, Ruchazie, on an April night in 1984 shocked the city, much used to murder and violence, in a way that has not been duplicated since.

Six members of the same "hard working and decent family" died in a fire deliberately set. But if this horrendous outcome was a surprise to most in the city it was no such thing to the police or many in the east end. Or even to those who had read their newspapers assiduously. Any initial view that the murders were motiveless, just another weekend scheme fire, soon evaporated. The cause was a vendetta, part of a battle for control of the ice cream vans that nightly toured the grim streets of the east end schemes. The cheery musical chimes that summoned youngsters from the close mouths to buy a "slider" (ice cream wafer) or "ginger" (fizzy drink) may have seemed innocent and, in the case of many of the legitimate traders, this was so. But the east end's hardened core of criminals saw ice cream vans in another light – vehicles for the distribution of drugs, stolen alcohol or cigarettes, or as a way of laundering money garnered in their criminal enterprises. In the wrong hands a fleet of ice cream vans represented an easy road to big money. Even on the right side of the law there were good profits to be made. Some operator/drivers had sales of around two thousand pounds a week – really good money in the eighties. But any ambitious gang leader anxious to build an empire based on the control of the vans in the schemes had first to clear out and frighten off the legitimate traders. That this was happening even before the horrors of Bankend Street was evident in a string of news reports of attacks on vans. As is usual in such cases some of the victims were reluctant to be identified, but one anonymous and "clean" operator spelled out the problem to the press in simple terms: he was attacked by an axe man at his garage and advised to leave the ice cream business if he wanted a long and healthy life. It was advice that the heavies who were nosing him up really meant. And advice that was difficult to refuse. Another operator Lorenzo Boni, from Bathgate, out on the road to Edinburgh, had a fleet of ice cream vans and was a Scottish representative of the Ice Cream Alliance who had traders on the streets in almost every city and town in Britain. He went along with the theory that a vendetta was responsible for the killings. He told of attacks on himself and his drivers involving bricks through windscreens, beatings, nails in tyres, sugar in petrol and road blocks. He took the hint. He sold up.

The family who died in the infamous blaze were the Doyles of Bankend Street. One of the six victims was young Andrew Doyle who had an ice cream van on the streets. Before the attack on his home young Doyle had an unpleasant foretaste of the dangers of the business – shots had been fired through the windscreen of his van, in which he was accompanied by a fifteen-year-old assistant. The men who plotted to take over the vans were no amateurs. They meant business.

Bankend Street, home to the extended Doyle family, was in Ruchazie, a sink estate with little to offer any decent family who found themselves housed there. So bad were the housing conditions that, notwithstanding a costly makeover by the council in an attempt to introduce even a smidgeon of community spirit, eventually the authorities decreed there was only one thing to do – call in the bulldozers. The sixty-four houses, once an eyesore, visible from the motorway by drivers coming in from the east, were battered out of existence and into history.

At the end the occupancy rate had dropped to fifty per cent and people were reduced to living alongside burned out flats and boarded windows. The anti-social tenants had beaten all attempts to improve life in the area. Money spent on new roofs, balconies and titivation generally was money down the sink. The vandals simply kept on destroying what remained of their own environment.

But whatever the difficulties of day to day life in such a place, before the horror of the fire, the folk of Bankend Street, like the Doyles, went about their business and family life as best they could. And fate was to play a cruel trick on the Doyles as they did so. On the night of the infamous attack their household was brimming over with family members celebrating the birth of a granddaughter days before. This ill-fated house party added to the death toll. Those who died were: James Doyle Snr, 53; James Doyle Jnr, 23; Tony Doyle, 14; Andrew Doyle, 18; their sister Christine Halleron, 25; and baby Mark Halleron, aged one.

The cause was, in the words of Detective Superintendent Norman Walker of the Glasgow CID, "a bloody murderous act". The Doyle's flat was a three-bedroomed home with an L-shaped corridor. There was a cupboard which the family had used to store timber and tyres and it was here the fire, which had been deliberately lit, had grown in intensity before literally exploding out, in a wall of flame, along the corridor to the bedrooms where the family slept. Nine people were trapped behind the flames that night. Mrs Lillian Doyle, 52, had been persuaded to jump from a window ledge and survived despite smoke inhalation injuries and shock. Two of her sons also survived. Stephen, 21, fled the flames and jumped 40 feet from a window ending up on the operating table in the Royal Infirmary with serious back injuries and a shattered leg. Daniel, 28, ended up in the burns unit of the Royal. Andrew, who also had serious burns, rallied briefly in the Royal, giving his tragic mother some hope that he, too, might survive, but relapsed and died.

By now the city was caught up yet again in the fever of a very public murder hunt. The fate of the Doyles and the implications of the vendetta that caused it were talking points from the posh salons of Kelvinside to the remaining tenements of the Gorbals. But there was less talking around the scene of the crime itself. The police faced that Glasgow cliché – "a wall of silence". That some sort of feud was involved was in no doubt. It emerged that young Andrew had not only been shot at prior to the fire – he had also been savagely beaten just after leaving his van parked outside his home.

In an attempt to get people in the area to talk, the police enlisted the help of the local *Evening Times* which produced a dramatic appeal poster that was distributed into every nook and cranny in the area. It worked and the police said citizens had come forward and that the poster had produced a few good lines of inquiry. All to the good, but the nasty side of Glasgow was also in evidence at this time. Shockingly police had to investigate bogus collectors knocking doors and collecting cash said to be for the stricken family, but money that went quickly down the dry throats of evil impostors. In a flurry of police activity – they were under terrific public pressure for action – there were arrests, charges made and charges dropped. Initially two men were accused of murdering the Doyles by setting fire to their home. Thomas Campbell, thirty-one, and Thomas Lafferty, eighteen, were remanded in custody at Glasgow Sheriff Court. The murder charges followed on to Campbell and Lafferty, who had already appeared in court accused of attempting to murder Andrew Doyle and fifteen-year-old Anne Wilson by firing a shot at them through the windscreen of their ice cream van. They also faced charges of plotting to build up an ice cream business by means of threats and intimidation. A few days later three other men were also charged. They were Joseph Steele, twenty-two, and Gary Moore, twenty-one, from Garthamlock and thirty-one-year-old Thomas Gray from Carntyne. The charge against the three men was that while acting with two others they wilfully set fire to a cupboard door and the entrance to the house. The fire took effect and the family residing there died as a result;

and they murdered them. The murder charge against Lafferty was later abandoned and in September 1984 Campbell, Gray, Moore and Steele went on trial in the High Court. The four accused denied the charges and lodged special defences of alibi and incrimination naming other persons.

The trial lasted twenty-seven days and in the end the jury was instructed by Lord Kincraig to return a not guilty verdict on the murder charge against Gray and the Crown dropped the case against Moore and cleared him because of insufficient evidence. The jury took eight hours to reach a verdict and Steele and TC Campbell were described as "vicious and dangerous" and given life sentences. For Campbell the judge ruled that life meant a minimum of twenty years in prison; no recommendation was made in the case of Steele. In addition Campbell was jailed for ten years after being found guilty of assault with intention to endanger the lives of Andrew Doyle and Anne Wilson during an armed attack on their ice cream van.

But all this was to turn out to be only an early chapter in a tale, unparalleled in Scottish legal history, which runs to this day.

Almost from the moment of his arrest Campbell protested his innocence. And has done so for more than twenty years. Campbell made no pretence that his background was not a criminal one – he had led the Gaucho on that night of terror in Haghill back in 1972, described earlier in this book, and his gang exploits, including bloody battles with the Powrie, had put him behind bars. As a gang leader he had led from the front, a powerful figure always in the thick of the action.

Incarcerated in Peterhead after the ice cream wars trial, Campbell was a difficult man. Peterhead seems to have suffered much in this way – it was there that Paddy Meehan spent much time wrongly accused and giving the staff major headaches.

Campbell had a passion for hunger strikes to underline his claims of innocence and he used his time to good effect to harass the authorities when he thought them in the wrong. He planned action in the European Court of Human Rights in connection with alleged interference with his mail and other infringements and won damages of £250 as compensation for the authorities allowing him to suffer an attack of bed bugs in his cell. He won a not guilty verdict on a charge of assaulting a prison officer and pursued a claim resulting from this incident against the then Secretary of State for Scotland, Malcolm Rifkind, and was awarded £4,000.

Steele, too, proclaimed his innocence and the pair made headlines over the years and became known as the Glasgow Two. They were already making legal history and Campbell added another footnote to the story of Scottish prisons in 1994 by being the last prisoner transferred out of the famous Barlinnie Special Unit.

The unit had attracted worldwide attention from penal reformers and has some spectacular successes in rehabilitation, like Jimmy Boyle and Hugh Collins who left villainy behind to become figures of stature in the art world. But at the end of its controversial life a working party concluded that it was no longer performing its function and it disappeared into legend. "TC" wasn't the only person to mourn its passing.

In 1995 Campbell and Steele had a brief taste of freedom on appeal before being returned to jail after a hearing of three senior judges turned down their submissions. But by late 2001 TC Campbell and Joseph Steele were back on the streets of Glasgow granted interim liberation by appeal court judges after a referral by the Criminal Cases Review Commission. This was the first step in the final vindication of the Glasgow Two. Their convictions were quashed in March 2004 when new evidence emerged to cast doubt on police statements at their original trial and Lord Gill, sitting with Lord Maclean and Lord McFadyen, overturned the finding of guilt and cleared them.

But even during interim liberation Campbell had not been able to stay out of the headlines. In his bad old days with the Gaucho "TC" was described as the self-styled Emperor of Carntyne and such a title inferred hardness. Proof of it surfaced again in spring 2002 when Campbell was attacked in the street in daylight by two men with "murderous intent", his own words, and he was whacked with a golf club. A trip to the hospital followed, but he was soon released claiming to feel "brand new".

This was not the only incident on the streets that spring. Tam McGraw was also attacked and had to be patched up in the private Ross Hall hospital, a somewhat more luxurious medical field station for the gangland wars than the casualty department of the Royal Infirmary where so many of Glasgow's leading criminal figures often found themselves.

And a certain John Paul Ferris was out of jail, back in again, and out again in a bewildering sequence of headlines and lurid newspaper stories.

Paul Ferris is, of course, the man who was so spectacularly cleared of acting with Bobby Glover and Joe "Bananas" Hanlon in the execution of Arthur Thompson Jnr. But his next court appearance produced a different result. He went down for seven years for gun-running, but only served half the sentence and reappeared in Glasgow in 2002, wallowing in press attention and telling anyone who would listen that he was a reformed character. But after the McGraw incident he was briefly back in prison and then released.

Ferris, who grew up in a criminal family in Blackhill, was always destined for a career at odds with the law. He was involved with several Glasgow crime empires but in the early days he worked for old Arthur Thompson and there were no complaints that this young hard man didn't both enjoy his work and carry it out with suitable ruthlessness and viciousness. He was a much feared figure in the east end, expert with baseball bat or knife. Old Arthur didn't employ patsies. Along the way Ferris gathered a group of nicknames from "Lucky" to "Baby Face" to "Wee Paul" and "Houdini", the latter a tribute to his ability to wriggle out of trouble. Mind you, I suspect that to call him Wee Paul to his face would be both brave and unwise. But just as the real Houdini, the original theatrical escape artist, in the end went too far, so justice caught up with Ferris.

In July 1998 he was found guilty of masterminding a shipment of guns and explosives, thought by some to be intended for Manchester's drug dealers who had a seemingly insatiable appetite for firearms. His arrest came after a massive two-year surveillance operation by detectives working for the National Crime Squad. In court Judge Henry Backsell said Ferris had "arranged, paid for and taken delivery of a lethal parcel of weapons". The judge said he could hardly dare to speculate on the potential for death and destruction they might have caused had they reached their intended destination. Paul Ferris is on record with complaints that he was too often the victim of police fit-ups and in his public pronouncements he seems paranoid about Strathclyde Police. But there was satisfaction in the ranks of the Glasgow bobbies who had seen so much of this enforcer's mayhem at close quarters that he was in jail, even in the south, for a long spell. Satisfaction, too, that intelligence from the city's detectives had played a role in his downfall.

But the Blackhill boy would take his own twisted satisfaction from the fact that his day in court was staged in London's Central Criminal Court, under the shadow of the figure of justice that crowns the dome of this most famous of buildings in the history of crime. And before he was sent north to Durham, nearer the scene of his early criminal life, he languished briefly in London's Belmarsh prison – nicknamed Helmarsh – a place that recently played host to such as Jeffrey Archer and Ronnie Biggs.

But, as is the way with British justice, a release for Ferris was only three and a half years away, just half of the sentence. He had originally been sentenced to ten years but the sentence was cut to seven at an Appeal Court sitting. Lord Justice Belden, sitting with Mr Justice Harrison and Mr Justice Lyas, reduced the term after making reference to a man who had supplied huge quantities of guns to some of the UK's most vicious criminals. Gun dealer Anthony Mitchell admitted charges of supplying weapons to crooks, including Ferris. He was handed down eight years at the Bailey. Lord Justice Belden said: "Bearing in mind the eight year sentence given to this man it is clear to us that the sentence imposed on Ferris is too high." This was a significant disappointment for those who had felt even ten years was not enough. And food for thought for Ferris's enemies who had now to reckon with a much earlier return of the would-be Godfather to his old haunts.

So the scene was set for a new chapter of warfare. All the ingredients were in place. Ferris out of jail, Tam McGraw, who tended to spend much time in the sunshine of Tenerife, back in the city for a spell. But there were surprises galore in store.

13

DAYLIGHT BATTERY

In the modern criminal era two strands of violence continue to blight Glasgow. The most recent crime figures available, autumn 2002, show a horrendous rise in what the tabloids call the culture of the blade, but which in more down-to-earth terms simply means that the war against knife-wielding thugs has clearly not been won. And that gangs running wild with weapons in an orgy of mindless violence can still terrify areas where honest folk have a right to a life of calm.

The measure of the size of the current problem is contained in figures provided by Scotland's Justice Minister Jim Wallace speaking in Glasgow at an international conference on crime. Strathclyde Police revealed that convictions for carrying knives had risen by 347 per cent since 1996. The very weekend the statistics were discussed by the conference two men died and five others were injured in separate attacks.

Alongside this festering sore on the city runs a different, but just as inescapable, battle. The ongoing battle of the big-time gangs, the drugs supremos.

This was at its most visible early in 2002 with factions struggling for control of drugs and territory clashing in broad daylight in the city streets. These gangs, the successors to Thompson and Norval rather than the Billy Boys or the Conks, pose a threat to vast areas of deprivation, growing rich on the drug trade and spreading the evil poison of addiction. But with a certain logical realism it can be pointed out that this sort of gangland violence rarely directly affects innocent people. With McGraw, Ferris and Campbell all making headlines about daylight whackings in the streets, Chief Superintendent Kevin Smith, divisional commander at the London Road police station, for many years a station as close to the front line as you could get, could tell the Press: "It is important to stress that these types of incidents generally involve a certain circle of people and not the community at large."

At the centre of that circle these days are undoubtedly Paul "Houdini" Ferris and Tam "The Licensee" McGraw. Their intertwined history is complex, going back to their days in the Barlanark Team and the Thompson empire. At one stage they both worked for Old Arthur, Glasgow's most infamous "retired business man", before going their separate ways. And, in the case of McGraw, building up a fortune reputed to be in the £10 million range. Recent events indicate some kind of truce between them, but at times they have been sworn enemies.

The details of the spring 2002 attacks are revealing. In April, McGraw even got his lawyers to issue a statement that he had not been repeatedly stabbed in the street attack, despite press reports, and was fit and well in his home. As mentioned in the previous chapter, TC Campbell was less reticent about another incident in which he was left with the imprint of a golf club in his head. He was attacked in Halhill Road near his Barlanark home and tried to fend his assailants off using his street fighting and boxing skills. "I got whacked on the head with a golf club as I tried to face the stabber. I managed to get the knife off him but they kept on coming at me." The attack "had come out of the blue. I had just got out of the house and got to the gate of the community centre [close to a primary school] when a car pulled up and two men jumped out with murderous intent". Campbell went on to say that he told the attackers: "Leave it out, look at the witnesses. You are going to jail. Don't be stupid." But the assault went on for around ten minutes with attackers and victims at times rolling on the ground. "My training as a boxer when I was younger helped me ward off and sidestep the blows. It definitely saved my life."

Such was street life in Glasgow more than a hundred years after the Penny Mob had first made a gangland mark on the city.

But the gangsters had another big surprise in store for newspaper readers horrified by this new eruption of public violence – a document that seemed to promise peace in our time for at least two of the big-time gangsters. The *Daily Record*, always quick on the case in gangland matters, trumpeted an astonishing exclusive story in gigantic front page headlines – "Contract of the Devils and Gangsters' Hitman Pact". The gist of it was that McGraw and Ferris had gone to a lawyer to draw up a document that would guarantee them both some form of personal safety in an underworld that was becoming too hot for everyone's comfort. The "sworn enemies" were said to have made a legal pact that safeguarded both their lives from underworld assassins. If either were to be killed, and the finger of suspicion pointed at the other, the survivor's interests would pass to the victim's associates. Straight out of a Hollywood "B" movie on the Mafia you might think, but this nonetheless had an underworld source telling the ever-perceptive *Record* that "the war was over". The deal was said to be valid for five years.

The businesses involved were said to include all sorts of properties, car valeting, a car hire company and leisure industry businesses including a city centre bar.

A police spokesman said: "This pair have been at each other's throats for years. It's pretty amazing if they have entered into an agreement like this."

History will deliver its verdict on this unusual turn of affairs. But there is more solid evidence of the ongoing inability to curb violence in Glasgow and Scotland generally in the latest crime figures as discussed in the Scottish Parliament, for the growth in knife-carrying is a blight on all Scotland's cities, not just Glasgow. As usual, there were attempts to turn the upsurge in blade crime into a political football – it has always been thus. The SNP asked Justice Minister Jim Wallace to release the details of convictions for carrying offensive weapons. They showed, as has been pointed out, that there was a massive rise. At the same time there has been a rise in successful convictions of almost 350 per cent in the same period.

The SNP claimed that Scotland faced an unprecedented upsurge in crimes involving knives and offensive weapons. Jim Wallace and the police took the view that the increase in convictions showed that the police had both the numbers and powers to deal with the growing problem of weapons crime. A view, however accurate, that is unlikely to provide comfort for someone robbed at knife-point. Jim Wallace highlighted the old Glasgow predilection for binge drinking as part of the problem. And top policemen pointed out that if you are in the habit of going around with a knife hidden on you and you end up in a drunken argument – sometime over matters of little significance – then there is the probability that you will use it, perhaps to lethal effect. The current rise in knife crime highlights the relative failure of such high profile initiatives by the police such as Operation Blade in 1993 and the more recent Spotlight Initiative. The police, often aided by the Press, throw enormous resources and effort into such schemes which seem to produce spectacular short-term success, but don't really stop the overall rise in weapons carrying. It is significant that although the problem has caught major public attention and been tackled in many different and imaginative ways, research conducted by Glasgow University's Professor Neil McKeganey shows that one in three boys and one in twelve girls across Scotland has carried a knife at some time. In the Spotlight Initiative blades were found hidden inside mobile phones. A child's lollipop stick was rigged up with carpet knife blades. A flick knife was disguised as a cigarette lighter and a sword and a pig splitter were taken from youths. A new academic study of knife culture is planned by the Scottish Executive and Strathclyde Police. Chief Constable Willie Rae has welcomed it: "This study is something that has never been done before. It will take a different look at why this issue is seen in such extremes in the West of Scotland. It is evident across the whole of Scotland but not in the extremes we see here in the west.

We need to understand why."

It is desperately dispiriting that despite all that has happened down the years the twin evils of street gangs and organised crime are still with us.

The SNP leader John Sweeney's comments resonate back to the twenties and thirties: "Scotland's police forces face an uphill struggle dealing with this desperately serious problem. What is required is a concerted effort to deal with the knife-carrying culture – especially among the young – and a real drive to punish those who flout the rules of civilised society.

"We need a twin track approach that puts resources into our communities aimed at keeping kids out of a life of crime, while at the same time taking hard core offenders off the streets." These are sentiments that could have come straight from the letters column of the *Glasgow Herald* more than fifty years ago. This book's chronicle of crime in the city underlines the fact that much of it is of a cyclical nature. Crime waves crash against the rocky shore of social awareness and conscience with sickening regularity. The belief that gangs and gangland grew out of social deprivation, the theory that they were the inevitable outcome of bad housing and unemployment, is sustainable up to a point in the twenties and thirties, and maybe even right up to the sixties and seventies when the home living conditions of the men who fought in the gangs was simply appalling. But even back then the comments of people like Billy Fullerton of the Brigton Billy Boys spelled out that there was more to it than simply living up a gas-lit close stinking with the smell of urine or sleeping and eating in overcrowded rooms with a four legged rat or two ready to take a nibble at your meat . . . running with a gang, the comradeship involved, the discipline, the control over a territory, were all factors that attracted men to gang life. Some of the old newspaper reports on "the thrill of being in a gang" touch a real cord. Academic studies throughout the world show that the excitement of being a gang member also attracts the relatively well off, the rebels who will not conform to family ideals, as well as the disenfranchised. In the days of the old

Gorbals gangs there were people like Peter Williamson, leader of the Beehive, said by contemporary reports to be both well spoken and well educated and who came from a respectable family. In the history of crime there are many examples of gang culture – and terrorism – attracting intelligent people. I would like to have a pound or so for every time I have been told of a hoodlum that if he had gone straight he had the charm, energy and intelligence to get to the top of almost any profession. These particular concluding musings came to me in surprising surroundings in the heart of the new Gorbals. If you want to study the physical regeneration of an area fighting back from a black past there is no better place than the New Gorbals of 2002. Especially sipping a Budweiser or other designer label beer (maybe even something as exotic as a Bacardi Breezer) in the reception lounge of the £5.5m Days Inn in Ballater Street. Not until recently would you have expected such style in a hostelry just yards away from Gorbals Cross. The American chain hotel stands proudly on what was once the site of rat-infested gas-lit tenements, haunted by gangs. Internally, with its discreet ceiling lighting and shining chrome bar, it is not much different from the Florida beach-side hotels now used regularly by Glasgow holidaymakers – who you sometimes suspect are not sure whether Rothesay or Millport still exist. It is a potent sign of the success of the New Gorbals. But it is not a lone icon: round the corner there are all the usual signs of yuppiefication, with new low-rise flats with halogen lighting, balconies and the latest minimal interior design. In this hotel, a breakthrough for the Gorbals, you can sit and sip and decide whether or not to go to the latest spectacular theatrical offering in the world famous Citizens theatre, a few yards from the Cross. Or maybe some *avant garde* production in one of the city centre club theatres just over the Albert Bridge on the north bank of the Clyde is more appealing. It's your choice. And it's a million miles away from the old image of the area, a place of blackened tenements, peeling paint, graffiti and hopelessness with the depressed and unemployed living on the edge in fear of the gangs. The sawdust-floored bars, the haufs and half pints and the shawly women with their jugs of cheap red wine are no more. Good. But all the more puzzling when contemplating the fact that gangland and the knife culture are currently at a new high. The clichéd cry of the leader writer and the legal bench down the years has been: something must be done, these evil men must be punished, these young folk must be weaned off crime.

But much has been done. Glasgow is now a city that rightly attracts tourists from round the world and will continue to do so. The problems of crime and safety on the streets have been put into some sort of perspective. No longer do the politicians try to sweep the crime problems of Glasgow, which in the words of Charles Gordon, leader of the city council, are "no different from every big city in the world", out of the sight of newspaper readers or watchers of the television news programmes. The conspiracy of silence has ended and that is a massive step in the right direction. The comparison with other big cities, particularly those in America, is apposite. Psychologist Dr Geoff Scobie, of Glasgow University has said: "The two major English speaking nations in the world, America and Britain, seem to be merging in their habits." Apart from the influence of American crime culture he believes that another factor is that these days youngsters can afford to drink and do drugs, which fuels their aggressive behaviour.

The "something that must be done" now seems to be acknowledged as being a complete re-education of potential young criminals in the reality of the consequences of their violence and the removal of the idea that somehow aggressive gang behaviour can provide a harmless quick fix or excitement. And attractive alternatives have to be put in place. All that is an ambition close to the heart of the many good folk in Glasgow and its surroundings, who have wrestled with the problem for almost a hundred years. It is a perplexing, perhaps unobtainable, goal. But many have struggled mightily towards it.

The compassion and courage of such Christian folk as Warnes and Murray in Bridgeton, Cameron Peddie in the Gorbals, Youngson in Easterhouse, is truly remarkable. Constable John

Nolan and Frankie Vaughan in Easterhouse, and others, who sought that holy grail of the reformers: keeping the kids off the street, finding work for idle hands and beating the defective attraction of running with a gang, will be long remembered. The countless social workers, the Boys Brigade officers and the Scout movement, the YMCA workers, the committed community police officers, have tirelessly striven after such ideals. Hopefully modern successors will always emerge to carry on the fight. And hopefully, they, like Cameron Peddie, who ministered all these years ago in the Gorbals, will retain their belief in their fellow man, and be neither toughened nor made cynical by what they find in life on the streets of Glasgow.

INDEX